LIZ LOCHHEAD

Liz Lochhead is a poet, playwright and occasional theatre director. She was born in Lanarkshire in 1947 and educated at Glasgow School of Art. Her collections of poetry include *Dreaming Frankenstein* and *The Colour of Black & White* (published by Polygon).

Her dozen original stage plays include *Blood and Ice*, *Mary Queen of Scots Got Her Head Chopped Off* and *Perfect Days* – the 'sister play' to *Good Things* – which is also published by Nick Hern Books. Her many stage adaptations, all published by Nick Hern Books, include versions of Molière's *Tartuffe* and *Miseryguts* (based on *Le Misanthrope*), Euripides' *Medea* and *Thebans* (adapted mainly from Sophocles' *Oedipus* and *Antigone*).

Liz lives in Glasgow and is currently writer-in-residence at, jointly, Glasgow University and Glasgow School of Art. She became the city's Poet Laureate in 2005.

Other Titles in this Series

Henry Adam
AMONG UNBROKEN HEARTS
THE PEOPLE NEXT DOOR

Caryl Churchill
BLUE HEART
CHURCHILL PLAYS: THREE
CHURCHILL: SHORTS
CLOUD NINE
A DREAM PLAY
  after Strindberg
FAR AWAY
HOTEL
ICECREAM
LIGHT SHINING IN
  BUCKINGHAMSHIRE
MAD FOREST
A NUMBER
THE SKRIKER
THIS IS A CHAIR
THYESTES *after* Seneca
TRAPS

Ariel Dorfman
DEATH AND THE MAIDEN
READER
THE RESISTANCE TRILOGY
WIDOWS

Riccardo Galgani
THE FOUND MAN
GREEN FIELD

Stephen Greenhorn
PASSING PLACES

Catherine Grosvenor
ONE DAY ALL THIS WILL
  COME TO NOTHING

Chris Hannan
ELIZABETH GORDON QUINN
SHINING SOULS

Iain F MacLeod
HOMERS
I WAS A BEAUTIFUL DAY

Tony Kushner
ANGELS IN AMERICA –
  PARTS ONE & TWO
HOMEBODY/KABUL

Liz Lochhead
MEDEA *after* Euripides
MISERYGUTS *after* Molière
PERFECT DAYS
THEBANS *after* Euripides
  and Sophocles

Linda McLean
RIDDANCE
SHIMMER

Conor McPherson
DUBLIN CAROL
McPHERSON:
  FOUR PLAYS
McPHERSON PLAYS: TWO
PORT AUTHORITY
SHINING CITY
THE WEIR

Arthur Miller
AN ENEMY OF THE PEOPLE
  after Ibsen
PLAYING FOR TIME

Rona Munro
IRON
YOUR TURN TO CLEAN
  THE STAIR & FUGUE

Imogen Stubbs
WE HAPPY FEW

Polly Teale
AFTER MRS ROCHESTER
BRONTË
JANE EYRE
  after Charlotte Brontë

Amanda Whittington
BE MY BABY
SATIN 'N' STEEL

Liz Lochhead

GOOD THINGS

NICK HERN BOOKS
London
www.nickhernbooks.co.uk

A Nick Hern Book

Good Things first published in Great Britain as a paperback
original in 2006 by Nick Hern Books Limited, 14 Larden Road,
London W3 7ST

Good Things copyright © 2006 Liz Lochhead

Liz Lochhead has asserted her right to be identified as
the author of this work

Cover design: Ned Hoste/2H

Typeset by Country Setting, Kingsdown, Kent CT14 8ES
Printed and bound in Great Britain by Biddles, King's Lynn

A CIP catalogue record for this book is available from
the British Library

ISBN-13   978 1 85459 854 7
ISBN-10   1 85459 854 6

Good Things was first performed by Borderline Theatre
Company, in association with the Byre Theatre, St Andrews
and Perth Theatre, at the Tron Theatre, Glasgow on Thursday
16 September 2004.

The production then toured to Eastgate Theatre and Arts
Centre, Peebles; Barrfields Theatre, Largs; Howden Park
Centre, Livingston; Lochside Theatre, Castle Douglas; Falkirk
Town Hall; MacRobert Theatre, Stirling; Gaiety Theatre, Ayr;
Arts Guild Theatre, Greenock; Carnegie Hall, Dunfermline;
Eden Court Theatre, Inverness; Cumbernauld Theatre; Brunton
Theatre, Musselburgh; The Palace, Kilmarnock; Byre Theatre,
St Andrews and Perth Theatre.

The cast was as follows:

ACTRESS ONE (SUSAN)	Annette Staines
ACTOR ONE (DAVID)	Vincent Friell
ACTRESS TWO	
(MARJORIE, DORIS, et al)	Molly Innes
ACTOR TWO (FRAZER, TONY, et al)	Kenneth Bryans

Director   Maureen Beattie
Designer   Finlay McLay
Lighting Designer   Simon Wilkinson

Thanks to Eddie Jackson at Borderline for the imaginative
and exceptionally extensive series of workshops on this script
and to all the different actors and directors who contributed
at various times.

Liz Lochhead

GOOD THINGS

For Marion Marshall – and The Girls

Characters

SUSAN LOVE, *forty-nine*
  played by ACTRESS ONE
DAVID, *fifty-one*
  played by ACTOR ONE

SCOTCH DORIS, *sixty-ish*
MARJORIE, *forty-five-ish*
WELL-DRESSED WOMAN
NATALIE, *thirty-two*
SHARP YOUNG POLICEWOMAN
HELENA, *twenty-two*
  all played by ACTRESS TWO

FRAZER, *forty-ish*
ARCHIE, *eighty-four*
TONY, *fifty-ish*
SCRUFFY LITTLE MAN, *sixty*
FLOWER DELIVERY MAN
INSENSITIVE POLICEMAN
  all played by ACTOR TWO

The fast and frequent changes effected by these second two actors are very much part of the audience's fun and enjoyment.

'Scotch Doris' is Scottish, obviously, and has a lot of strongly idiomatic dialogue – but Susan could well be too, albeit with only a Scots accent on her perfectly standard English vocabulary and syntax.

The town, or big city suburb, could be anywhere, but the scene is the little charity shop on the corner – very much Frazer's designer-palace – on three different days in one year.

There should be as miraculous and swift a transformation as possible between Act One, 6 January, and Act Two, Valentine's Day.

Act Three should have a very different Christmas tree and decorations from Act One.

Possibly on one of the three days (perhaps Act One?), it is pouring with rain outside, and people come in from the outside wet. A cold dry bright winter's day for Act Two would therefore contrast beautifully.

ACT ONE

TWELFTH NIGHT (*Farce*)

Music: 'Time is On My Side' (Rolling Stones), loud.

*6 January. A little charity shop on the corner. The rather
spectacular Christmas decorations are more than half down
but a last section on one side is very much still to do. There's
the A-frame of an open step-ladder and under it a full box
spilling gorgeously coloured tinsel.*

*Stage right, on the back wall, there is a doorway to backshop
with a door, currently closed, clearly marked 'Private'.*

*Stage left, on the back wall, behind a single full-length front
curtain, currently closed, there are two slightly angled, adjoining,
tiny changing-room spaces, each with a curtain stopping well
short of the floor, which shows the legs and feet, though covers
the heads, if and when the long front curtain is open.*

The shop's front door entrance/exit from street is stage left.

FRAZER, *a dapper man in early middle age and* SUSAN,
*attractive, warm, likeable, youthful-looking for her late forties,
stand near each other, poised.* FRAZER *is looking at his
watch, waiting for the second hand to reach the twelve. He
points at* SUSAN: *Go!* SUSAN *takes a deep breath, then –*

SUSAN. OK, what I'll say, I'll say: Susan. Friendship. Friendship
and fun really. Nothing too serious! Susan Love –

(But you know, Frazer, I'm seriously thinking of reverting
to my maiden name, only I've not used it for so long –
obviously it's not me, though what is? I mean, there could
be pluses, well, in the self-esteem department? I suppose.)

My counsellor suggested it, that the time would come I
might feel that taking back my own name would be
appropriate – not that I go in much for therapy or
counselling or stuff – but he was helpful. Definitely.

I thought, avail yourself of everything, Susan, everything that's going – and it was part of a package at work, my friend Mel that's just moved to Macclesfield with her husband, she recommended it, she said, 'Susan, see a counsellor, I would, it's free, there's no shame, did wonders for me with that second miscarriage before little Benny was born when I just couldn't see light at the end of the tunnel, he's very good, he helps you get in touch with your feelings.'

I said, 'Mel, I've got no problem feeling my feelings, I wish I could stop feeling them, I'm awash with the bloody things.' She said, 'I know but he helps you accept your grief and move through it, realise you're not always going to feel like this and, well, put it in perspective sort of thing. You know . . . grieve and move on?'

I said, 'I don't know if *grief's* what I'd call it exactly' but – he helped! Oh, it was only the six free sessions, no way would I or could I ever get into that sort of self-indulgence and expense long-term.

And I'm fine. D'you know, eighteen months on, some days I feel quite excited. Exhilarated. A clean slate. Hence ditch the Love, though why should I change the person I've been for the last twenty-four years because my husband ups sticks? And it's my daughter's name, so I'm probably stuck with Love for the duration.

FRAZER (*tapping watch, c'mon!*). Sus-ann!

SUSAN. Right what? God . . . My interests? Macrame, origami and aqua-nooky!

Well . . . Music. All sorts. Stones, Sinatra, Springsteen, Sibelius. Ella, anybody good! Except folk. Folk or jazz. Can't stand jazz, too jangly. Nor can I abide dance or house or rap. None of the stuff that our Stephi drives me up the wall with. Easy listening? I find that hard to take.

Love going to the pictures! Just about anything. Old black-and-whites on the telly on a Sunday afternoon –

FRAZER. Time's up.

SUSAN. Really? That's what I'm afraid of. Game over.

FRAZER. Why?

SUSAN. Past it. That's me! Most probably. Face it, Frazer, I'm forty-eight, forty-nine in February.

FRAZER. Yes, but you don't need to tell them that!

SUSAN. Why not? It's the truth. This year I'll be hitting my fiftieth year.

FRAZER. Is fifty not supposed to be the new thirty?

SUSAN. – The full half-century. How the hell did that happen?

DORIS, *a regular, sixty-ish, known as 'Scotch Doris', sticks her head round one side of the changing-room area's front curtain.*

DORIS. You don't look it, darlin'. Do you have this in a size bigger?

FRAZER. Perhaps 'modom' would prefer it in the aubergine? This is a *charity* shop, Doris! All one-offs, obviously. Duh!

DORIS *sweeps the front curtain wide open and emerges. She looks a fright in whatever (much too tight).*

Stage-right cubicle's short curtain is shut, no legs showing in there, it's clearly empty. DORIS's stage-left cubicle has its short curtain wide open. She has a colourful half of the shop's stock in there to try on.

DORIS. Mibbe I could let the darts out?

FRAZER *rolls his eyes.*

Mibbe I could put in a gusset up the back in a contrast fabric or make an insert out of an elastic placket and wear it under a cardigan?

FRAZER. Doris –

DORIS. Anybody haufweys handy with a Singer could save themselves a pure fortune in here.

FRAZER. Doris, did you try the navy?

DORIS. Don't know that I fancy it.

FRAZER. Try it. For me!

DORIS *sighs and indulges him, disappears back into the inner-curtained cubicle.* SUSAN *pulls across the full-length outer curtain for (her own) privacy's sake.*

SUSAN. When did *she* come in?

FRAZER *shrugs.*

Did you know she was in there?

FRAZER. I forgot.

He scuttles back up the stepladder to demolish more decorations.

SUSAN. Honestly! I'm back there sorting out the post-Christmas-unwanted-present mountain into some sort of order for Her Majesty Marjorie to price when she deigns to come in, I back through here, you don't even bother to tell me there's someone in the changing room and we are Not Alone.

Could've been anybody! But, oh, you've got to get me – Ooh!

Laughing, she throws a cushion from the soft-furnishings pile. He chucks it back.

FRAZER. – Practicing your sales pitch for the speed dating. Tonight! Which was hopeless to be perfectly frank and honest.

SUSAN. Really?

Listen, not a *word* to Marjorie about this! I don't want her to start trying to fix me up with one of Douglas's golfing cronies again. Spare me. Please!

Was I really so rubbish? What should I say?

FRAZER. Well, skip the past for a start! Forget it. Just . . . answer those questions I asked you in the first place: 'Who are you? And what do you want to get out of this?' Sell yourself, Susan. You're a lovely lady.

SUSAN. No point in telling any lies. This is it. Here I am. What you see is what you get.

God! Sell myself? I don't think I could give myself away.

Snogging? Couldn't! What do you do with your face? Do you pucker up or open up?

FRAZER, *up the top of the ladder, holds out a sprig of mistletoe above her and puckers up, eyes shut. She snatches it, bins it, laughing.*

Hey! Hey, you know how my old dad's in his second childhood? I think I've hit my second adolescence. It's exactly the same as the first time. I can't conceive of anyone of the opposite sex treating me as a sexual being.

Or what the hell I'd do if they did.

FRAZER *takes down the last tinsel.*

FRAZER. There's more to life, Susan! (There better be, says me!)

He comes down the ladder.

Hey! Remember how you were saying you fancy trying that salsa dancing? There's a class advertised up the sports centre. Beginners. Let's give it a shot, mmm?

SUSAN. Why not! You never know, I might meet my ideal man – don't they tell you to try evening classes? (Mind you, I'm not stupid, all you ever meet are other women looking for their ideal man . . .)

But let's give the salsa a whirl! The worst that could happen is we learn to dance.

He gives her a whirl and backwards dip, copied from the telly.

FRAZER. Absolutely! I might not be your ideal partner, missus, but I'm keen!

SUSAN (*laughing*). And it was our new year resolution that we'd try something new . . .

SUSAN sits at the counter, fishes a book out from her handbag, opens it, starts reading, so now talks automatically, distractedly.

FRAZER. So it was. Ooh, hope this is a good year for us, eh? Here's hoping we each get our heart's desire.

Nice if we could both move on and get out of here, eh, the pair of us?

SUSAN. Any chance of anything?

FRAZER. Well, there's a movie I heard about, supposed to be definitely going to go in the spring, fingers crossed, director I did the frocks for, for his first costume epic at the Beeb in '87 for two and six on an education and documentary budget, so you'd think I'd be in with a chance there. I e-mailed my CV but quite honestly the so-called 'producers' these days are about twelve-and-a-half years old, the lot of them.

SUSAN (*automatic*). I suppose it's Who You Know . . .

FRAZER. And of course with what I went through with my mother, I've let myself fall out of the loop somewhat. Oh, no regrets! (*Kisses fairy and dumps her.*) Well, there's the Christmas-tree fairy back in her box for another year, aren't you, pet?

Well, Frazer son, what theme are you going to use for the window dressing this month, eh? Should I skip straight to Valentine's? WH Smith has already!

What you reading?

Grabs it, she grabs it back, reads.

SUSAN. *Doctor Zhivago*. I'm getting into it. Course, nothing could touch the film. Remember Julie Christie and Omar Sharif and at the end they just kept passing each other and missing – Oh, it was so romantic. Not a dry eye in the two and nines. Certainly not mine!

FRAZER. I'm not a big reader.

SUSAN. Stephi bought me it for my Christmas last Christmas and I only got round to finally starting it this Christmas because the TV was so utterly appalling.

FRAZER. Wasn't it just? Have you no work to do?

SUSAN. No. Give me a break, I'm at a good bit. Put the kettle on, go on.

He blows a kiss and indulges her, then goes backshop.

SUSAN *reads. From cubicle comes some harrumphing and groaning.* SUSAN *registers it, ignores it. It gets louder.*

DORIS *(off)*. Haw! Am I supposed tae tie masel in knots like Houdini in here? Is there naebody can gie me a wee haun wi these press-fasteners?

SUSAN. Certainly, Doris, certainly. Your servant, I'm sure.

SUSAN *fashions herself a bookmark, places it, sighs, shuts book, goes behind the front curtain.*

A very scruffy little MAN *enters, stands, surveys the empty shop imperiously, then nods to himself.*

MAN. Right . . .

SUSAN *comes out of cubicle.*

SUSAN. Ah! Sir, can I – ?

MAN. Old things, eh?

SUSAN. Many with a lot of good wear in them! For instance this overcoat would –

MAN. No, no, I'm not *buying.*

DORIS *(off)*. Well, you can beat it well!

The scruffy MAN *looks amazed.*

MAN *(to* SUSAN*)*. Are you throwing your voice?

DORIS *sticks her head out from the long front curtain.*

DORIS. Because you'll be getting bugger all buckshee by the way! All the money's in a good cause!

MAN. Who asked you for your tuppenceworth?

He exits.

SUSAN. Now Doris, you've no call to go insulting our customers!

DORIS. Him! He was mingin'. He was honkin'. From here!

Your trouble is you've got too much time for timewasters. You shouldnae give them the time of day!

SUSAN. You never said a truer word. So, Doris, how was your Christmas?

DORIS. Very quiet.

SUSAN (*commiserating*). Well . . .

DORIS. I've got high hopes for this New Year, but!

SUSAN. Ever the optimist, eh?

DORIS. Like yoursel'!

SUSAN (*doubting it*). Am I?

DORIS. Oh aye! See, the good thing about getting to our age, you get to the 'Know Thyself' stage. Or you should, anyway.

Optimist rather than pessimist, extrovert no introvert, ectomorph, no, mesamorph, that's me!

DORIS *disappears behind the curtain.*

Laughing, SUSAN *makes for her book. Picks it up again and reads.* FRAZER *appears from backshop, wanders, catches sight of something out of the window out front.*

FRAZER. There she is! Here she comes . . .

SUSAN *gives up, shuts her book and leaves it on the counter, gets up and joins him, looking out.*

SUSAN. No rest for the wicked! Oh, don't park the Beamer there, Marjorie, or else you'll get a ticket and we'll never hear the end of it.

FRAZER. Oh my. She's talking to that horrible woman that owns Scandalrags next door.

SUSAN. So she is!

FRAZER *scurries to put the stepladders away backshop, then quickly reappears.*

(*Shouts.*) Doris, have you ever maxed out the plastic and bought yourself a dressy little frock out of Scandalrags?

DORIS (*off*). Oot o' whit?

SUSAN. The posh dress shop next door!

DORIS (*off*). I wouldn't give stuff out of their houseroom!

SUSAN. Oh I would . . . I would! (*To* FRAZER.) Apparently, Natalie shops in Scandalrags, according to our Stephi.

FRAZER. She would.

SUSAN. Oh, don't get me started!

FRAZER. Oh look . . . Oh no! Marjorie's getting stuff out of the boot, uh-oh, I see Tupperware . . .

SUSAN. Marjorie, please don't bring us in your post-Christmas glut! Remember last year, Frazer? We were up to here with your surplus panettone. We were pâtéd out. Let's tell her she can stick her stinky old stilton!

Oh, I know I shouldn't take the piss out of Marjorie, she means well, I love her dearly. She's got a good heart, Frazer. A helluva good heart.

It's just you really have to be feeling stout-hearted yourself to be up to it.

Enter MARJORIE, *a middle-class matron in her mid-forties, through the shop door.*

MARJORIE. Morning, Frazer!

FRAZER. Morning, Marjorie! Happy New Year!

He helps her with her Tupperware, taking it from her.

MARJORIE. You too!

FRAZER. Want a cuppa? Kettle's on.

FRAZER *exits backshop.*

MARJORIE. Morning, Susan, Happy New Year! My, it's marvellous to be out of that madhouse! Douglas and the boys are adorable, particularly when their chums are in and out like that – it's a hoot, but it's hard work!

Have you ever felt you can just get too much socialising?

SUSAN. Morning, Marjorie.

MARJORIE. Oh, I'm sorry, Susan, that was tactless of me. How was your Christmas? Did Stephi spend it with you . . . or was she with her dad and er . . . ?

SUSAN. Natalie. No, Marjorie – Tony and the famous Natalie, they spent Christmas in the sun somewhere. Stephi told me where but I can't remember, I wasn't interested, could it have been the Caribbean? Anyway, Stephi – very much on sufferance as she made bloody clear – was with me. And her old grandad, of course, who frankly didn't know if it was New Year or New York but what's new? Anyway, overall it was a fairly continent Christmas so we have to be grateful for small mercies.

MARJORIE. I'm full of admiration, so I am, Susan. I think you're marvellous. Out of the blue, your husband just up and offs with the younger woman, leaving you with the stroppy adolescent, during the following year you sell your house and move in with your old dad because he's no longer coping, you get made redundant – any single one, far less all these things together, are supposed to be Big Stressful Life Events, some of *the most* stressful – but you, you just take it all in your stride, you're not bitter, you're always exactly the same, you've got a smile for everybody –

SUSAN. Marjorie, have you seen all the super stuff that's come in?

MARJORIE. – I think you're marvellous, I really do!

SUSAN. I really think you should take a peek –

MARJORIE (*mildly irritated*). Oh, I will do. I've just got in the door!

SUSAN. – because there are some really good things!

MARJORIE. Well, excellent! (*Confides.*) Joanne from Head Office is coming in later to check my pricing policy. They are trying to standardise across the branches. As far as is feasible.

Enter TONY *through the shop door, a conspicuously youthfully well-dressed, fiftyish man* (*the type who has a young girlfriend*).

TONY. Susan.

SUSAN. For God's sake, what do you mean coming here, disturbing me at my work?

TONY. I was passing – you won't so much as talk to me on the phone if I've not made an appointment.

I want you to get Stephi to see sense.

MARJORIE. Do you need any help, Susan?

SUSAN. No thanks, Marjorie, I'm fine. Could you, eh, give us a bit of privacy?

MARJORIE. Oh certainly, Susan, sorry I spoke. You're sure you're OK?

MARJORIE *reluctantly goes through to backshop.*

SUSAN. Nice tan, Tony.

TONY. Thank you, Susan.

SUSAN. Listen, what the hell do you mean by –

MARJORIE *pokes her head out from backshop.*

MARJORIE. Because if That One gives you any bother, Susan –

SUSAN. Marjorie, I'm fine! Stephi to see sense about what?

TONY. You know very well what.

SUSAN. Enlighten me.

TONY. Don't try and pretend you never put her up to it.

SUSAN. Up to what?

TONY. Because it's just like you to pressurise her into refusing to come to the wedding.

SUSAN. Whose wedding?

TONY. She'll not even talk to me on the phone.

SUSAN. Whose wedding?

TONY. Don't you try and make out Stephi didn't tell you Natalie asked her to be her bridesmaid?

SUSAN. No. No, she never did.

TONY. It'll have been your attitude that made her scared to bring it up.

SUSAN. No, Tony, not so. But I think you could have told me. Yourself.

TONY. You've made it very clear you don't want to discuss anything with me except the welfare of our daughter.

SUSAN. That's true. And I don't. If Stephi doesn't want to be a bridesmaid at your wedding, you'll just have to take no for an answer.

TONY. That's nice! Well, tell Stephi from me that it goes two ways. She'll learn that if she don't play ball with me, I won't be playing ball with her either, OK?

Exit TONY.

SUSAN (*after him*). Oh, you and your balls, you stupid, stupid – Clear off! You're good at that.

SUSAN *sits down, weeping in anger.* MARJORIE, *coat off now, stands in entrance from backshop looking down, shaking her head. She approaches and touches* SUSAN's *arm, full of sympathy.*

MARJORIE. Susan . . .

SUSAN. Leave it, Marjorie, please!

MARJORIE. Poor you, Susan, what a –

SUSAN. Don't!

MARJORIE. Unbelievable! I heard every word . . .

SUSAN. I was afraid you would.

MARJORIE. You're better off without him, pet.

SUSAN *breathes deep, pulls herself together as best she can.* MARJORIE's *eyes widen as she catches sight of something through the front window.*

SUSAN. That would seem to be the general consensus.

MARJORIE. – I don't believe it! (*Making for the door.*) Oh, they're absolute 'B's – excuse my French.

Hello, excuse me, that's mine!

Exit MARJORIE *out of the front door. From off, as she goes:*

And I tried to get a ticket but the blinking machine's not working!

SUSAN *wipes eyes, breathes deep.*

SUSAN. Well, Marjorie, if there's anyone could get the better of a parking warden, it's you.

Oooh! That's right, Marjorie, you just tell them! Don't take it lying down! Do your stuff!

Immediately, the same little scruffy MAN *enters again through front door with a heavy binbag. He drags it up to desk and dumps it.*

MAN. So, you take stuff?

SUSAN. Depends. What sort of stuff?

Nothing electrical –

MAN. There might be a couple of electric things in there.

SUSAN. We're not allowed. For safety reasons.

MAN. S'all right, they're not working.

Enter a meek, nicely-dressed WOMAN.

SUSAN (*to* MAN). But –

The WOMAN *begins rifling through clothes and immediately finds both a dress and a raincoat.*

MAN. Just you chuck them out, my dear, if they're no use to you. Clothes! Old clothes. Plenty more. Lots more stuff. I'm clearing out. Moving house.

WOMAN. Excuse me, can I try these on?

SUSAN (*to* MAN). Yes, but you see actually – (*To* WOMAN.) Certainly, no problem. Just –

SUSAN *pulls back the right side of the long outer curtain and shows the* WOMAN *into the clearly empty cubicle next to the one where we saw* DORIS. *Now the* WOMAN's *feet in her smart shoes and the bottom of her legs are still clearly visible as she draws the short inner curtain over.*

MAN (*exiting*). I'll bring you the other stuff in soon, OK?

A harrumphing noise from DORIS *in her* (*currently curtained-over*) *side.*

SUSAN (*of the binbag*). Ooh! (*Beat.*) You all right in there, Doris?

SUSAN *pulls back the outer curtain in the stage-left changing room so we can see* DORIS*'s legs and boots, struggling in a pair of red-and-white spotted cotton trousers. We can now see two pairs of legs (*DORIS*'s and the* WOMAN*'s) and two pairs of moving elbows behind the closed inner curtains.*

DORIS (*off*). I'll just have to unfankle my feet oot this perr of pedalpushers. I should of perhaps took ma buits aff first.

SUSAN. Take your time, take your time, Doris, nobody's rushing you –

WOMAN (*off*). Excuse me, can you possibly give me a hand with this zip?

SUSAN. Certainly.

SUSAN *goes in to help the* WOMAN. *She closes the full-length outer curtain as she steps inside. For a nanosecond there's an empty stage.*

FRAZER*'s head pops out of the backroom entrance.*

FRAZER. Tea's up! Where is everybody?

Puzzled, FRAZER *goes backshop again.*

SUSAN *comes out and goes towards the* MAN*'s bag trepidatiously and gingerly looks inside. She recoils.*

SUSAN. Oh well, saved you hiring a skip!

FRAZER *enters from the backroom with his outdoor coat on.*

FRAZER. Oh, there you are. Where's Marjorie?

SUSAN. Traffic wardens.

FRAZER. Right. (Do they know who they're messing with?) Listen, my Number One New Year Resolution, Susie Q, is No More Marvel, we deserve better –

FRAZER *heads for the front door crossing with* MARJORIE *entering as he exits.*

So I'm just away for a pint of proper milk, ladies!

Tea's made, Marjorie! Through there!

Oooh . . . Perhaps a Belgian biscuit out of Rockingham's and break New Year Resolution Number Two?

Exit FRAZER.

MARJORIE (*after him*). Thanks, Frazer, you're a sweetheart! So he is, eh, Susan?

SUSAN. Yes, Frazer's lovely!

MARJORIE. Does he have a friend?

SUSAN. Stacks and stacks of them.

MARJORIE. No, I mean –

SUSAN. I know exactly what you mean and I don't know. No one live-in anyway, nobody he talks about particularly.

MARJORIE. There's an awfully nice chap in Douglas's office, nice type, as they say a confirmed bachelor, I wonder –

SUSAN. Marjorie, leave the boy alone! Frazer's perfectly happy how he is!

MARJORIE. If you say so.

SUSAN. I do!

MARJORIE *looks out of the window.*

MARJORIE. Blooming parking attendants! There they go, harassing some other innocent motorist. Ugly uniform, isn't it? Ugly job. I was just in time out there. They'd not actually started writing out the ticket.

MARJORIE *spots the bag of rubbish.*

What's this?

SUSAN. Don't ask, Marjorie, just go and get your tea, you've had a stressful experience.

MARJORIE. I'll give these so-and-sos a stressful experience all right! Blinking Little Hitlers!

MARJORIE *exits backshop.*

SUSAN. Oh I know Marjorie, I know . . .

SUSAN *looks down at the disgusting bag, dispirited. She looks in again, then ties the top of it back up firmly, shaking her head. The meek, well-dressed* WOMAN *comes out, and twirls in front of the mirror in her coat, preening herself almost apologetically.*

(*Of bag.*) Completely and utterly dis-bloody-gusting!

WOMAN. Sorry?

SUSAN. – Absolutely stinking!

WOMAN. Pardon?

SUSAN (*leaving bag*). No! Sorry . . . I . . .

WOMAN. I was just saying, what do you think of it? Really?

Scruffy MAN *comes in dragging another bag.*

SUSAN (*to* WOMAN). Very nice!

MAN. Oh, it's no bother! Phwaugh! I'm done in. This is even heavier than the last one . . .

SUSAN *whirls to stop him, bumping into and tripping over the first bag.*

SUSAN. Sir! At the moment we really are overstocked, so –

WOMAN. But you know, I don't know if it's really me . . .

The WOMAN *goes back into the changing room.* SUSAN *gets up. The* MAN *leaves his second bag and exits.*

MAN (*calling*). I've more. Plenty more where that came from! I'll be back!

SUSAN. Sir! Sir! We can't –

SUSAN *runs towards the second bag but he's gone. She speaks through the inner curtain to well-dressed* WOMAN.

What about the dress then? Was that any use?

The WOMAN*'s arm comes through the inner curtain, handing the dress over.* SUSAN *takes it.*

WOMAN. No . . . no . . . I'm not sure . . .

As SUSAN *walks by the second bag, she's hit by a whiff.*

SUSAN. Oh, what a smell!

WOMAN (*off*). Sorry?

SUSAN. No. No. Sorry, not you!

SUSAN hangs up the dress, goes back and bends to the second bag.

The WOMAN comes out of the changing room holding the coat on a hanger, all her attention on it, not looking at SUSAN, shaking her head at the sight of herself.

WOMAN. No. No, d'you know, I don't really think so . . .

SUSAN (*shouting at bag*). We're not a bloody rag-and-bone shop, you know!

WOMAN. No, no! I just mean I don't –

SUSAN. Oh, not you! Sorry, is it no use?

The worm turns.

WOMAN (*very brusquely*). No! No, it is not!

The WOMAN thrusts the coat on its hanger at SUSAN and exits through front door in high dudgeon.

SUSAN. That's nice!

(*Of the coat.*) Here, that *is* nice! This is a good thing. It really is fantastic quality. Astonishing what some folk chuck out, it really is! And weatherproof! Wonder if our Stephi would wear that? It's very smart. So I don't suppose she'd be seen dead in it.

MARJORIE *shouts out from backshop.*

MARJORIE (*off*). Are you not having any tea then, Susan?

SUSAN. Oh yes indeedy. In a mo, Marjorie.

SUSAN *puts the coat back on the rail, shouts.*

(*Shouts.*) How you doing in there, Doris?

DORIS (*off*). Ach, I don't think this is my lucky day!

SUSAN. Yours neither, eh?

Marjorie! Marjorie, we've got a Code Three here. Situation Red Alert! Toxic Waste.

There's a couple of bags here. Well, obviously we'll have to go through them . . .

Enter MARJORIE *from backshop.*

MARJORIE. Who brought them in?

SUSAN. A scruffy little sod.

MARJORIE. Well, Susan, you should've known not to accept them. You just say – politely but firmly – thanks very much! Thanks but no thanks!

SUSAN. Well, we will have to go through them now, because, as Frazer says, you never know the minute. (The clothes, no, but there could be valuable bric-a-brac. Has happened!) But I'll tell you one thing, it's not a task for anybody without their Marigolds, Marjorie.

MARJORIE *sees something out of the window.*

MARJORIE. Is that him? There's a man coming across the road with a big bag . . .

SUSAN. Sorry, Marjorie, you deal with it! I'm going to wash my hands and get a cuppa.

SUSAN *drags the two heavy, smelly bags behind her towards backshop.*

MARJORIE. – Because I'll give him short shrift!

MARJORIE *bends down behind the counter.*

DAVID, *an attractive man of about fifty, enters to the sight of* SUSAN *disappearing as she hums a few bars from the theme tune to* Steptoe & Son.

DAVID. Em . . . !

But the swing doors shut on him: 'Private'.

Ah!

As he looks round, MARJORIE *pops up behind the counter, her hands up with rubber gloves on, and an insane smile on her face.*

MARJORIE. Can I help you?

FRAZER *enters with a pint of milk and box of cookies, to see –*

DAVID. Well, I just . . .

MARJORIE. No, thank you!

> MARJORIE *picks up* DAVID*'s bag and runs with it to the door where she dumps it unceremoniously outside. She comes back and glares.*

> FRAZER, *amazed, dumps the milk and cookies beside* SUSAN*'s book on the desk, goes out, picks the bag back up, and brings it in again.*

FRAZER. Can I give you a hand, Marjorie?

DAVID. I have some things and I wondered if you –

MARJORIE (*beady*). Are they good things?

DAVID. Yes. Yes, I think so. If –

FRAZER. You *sure* I can't give you a hand, Marjorie?

MARJORIE. No, it's OK, Frazer, thank you!

> FRAZER *opens the bag, pulls out from the top an elegant classic and simple dress which he holds up against himself with a flourish.*

Oh, that –

MARJORIE *and* FRAZER (*in unison*). – is beautiful!

DAVID. It's just . . . Well, there's a couple of these dresses and coats and ladies jackets and so on. Good quality, so I thought –

MARJORIE. Oh excellent! (*Sympathetic.*) Have you had a bereavement?

> FRAZER *grabs* MARJORIE *and drags her away.*

FRAZER. For God's sake, Marjorie! Obviously the man's had a bereavement. Either that or he's a bloody transvestite!

> *He goes to* DAVID, *touches his arm.*

Did you lose your mother? Oh, I know how you feel. I lost mine more than two years ago and I'm still not right, am I, Marjorie?

DAVID. My wife actually. She died. Almost a year ago. I thought it was time to –

MARJORIE. Oh absolutely!

DAVID. And it's a waste.

MARJORIE. Oh absolutely.

DAVID. Somebody should be getting the good –

MARJORIE. Oh absolutely.

FRAZER. Marjorie! Why don't you go through and join Susan
   in that cup of tea that must be getting freezing cold by now!

   *FRAZER thrusts the pint of milk and the box of biscuits at
   her. She takes them, and exits with the dress over her arm to
   backroom, her embarassment dawning on her.*

   She's got a heart of gold! She really has.

DAVID. Seemed quite a character.

FRAZER. She is. She's a good woman. Really. Can I help you
   with anything else?

DAVID. No thanks.

   *He goes to leave but FRAZER puts his hand on his arm,
   detaining him.*

FRAZER. The charity will make a lot from your kind donation
   – we do charge proper economic prices, you know. They
   don't go for fifty pence! Never! And you know what a good
   cause . . .

   Not to speak of the pleasure it'll be for me to have some
   really classy stuff to work with. Unless that is – are you
   local? You're not, are you? Say you're not!

DAVID. Couldn't be more so, I'm just across the road!

FRAZER. Well, then no way, Mr . . .

DAVID. David.

FRAZER (*shaking his hand*). Frazer! How'd you do, David!
   Well, you see, there is generally a policy of swapping, so
   that the goods you brought will be sold in another branch
   and some of their best stock will come to us. It's a courtesy
   thing, you know, so you won't be distressed by seeing your
   wife's things –

DAVID. No. No, that wouldn't bother me at all. Christine's done with them now.

I mean, we sorted through everything, gave it all away just after she died, but I must have missed that cupboard in the spare bedroom – I was looking for my badminton racquet and there they all were! You know, I don't think she'd ever worn half of them. There was this pair of shoes, look, here, I found them still in the box! Think she must've bought these for our son's wedding then ended up in something comfier so she could dance the night away. And she sure did!

He pulls out a shoebox, and leaves it on the counter.

FRAZER. Well, we're always very grateful for good stock.

DAVID. She had a lot of style, my wife, she loved clothes but . . . She was a really practical person, you know? She hated waste, she was very green, a great recycler – I was always in her bad books for putting glass in the plastic bin or plastic in with glass!

She always made me laugh! Oh – !

He gestures his embarrassment at 'going on like this', and turns to go.

FRAZER (*decisively*). David. David, don't go away. There's a number I want to give you. It's in my address book through the back. Bear with me –

DAVID (*indicating door, he's in a hurry*). Frazer, I'm –

FRAZER. Please!

DAVID. OK.

FRAZER exits to backroom.

DAVID idly picks up SUSAN's Doctor Zhivago, looks at it, whistles 'Lara's Theme' from the film, smiles, and decides to buy it.

He crouches down to rifle through a small heap of books on the downstage side of the counter as SUSAN enters from the backroom. They are both hidden from each other's sight.

SUSAN *is carrying the good dress that* DAVID *brought to the shop. It's on a hanger and prominently priced by* MARJORIE. *She gives a little twirl as she passes the mirror, holding it up to herself.*

SUSAN. No, Susan, sweetheart, definitely not for you!

She hangs it up and is exiting again, just as DAVID, *hearing her and about to ask her something stands up. But she's gone. He puts another book on top of* Doctor Zhivago, *obscuring it.*

FRAZER *enters, holding out a piece of paper with a number on it.*

DAVID. Didn't know you did books.

FRAZER. Books, vinyl – oh, those down there, they've still to be sorted and shelved.

DAVID. This *Halliwell's Film Guide* is a lot more recent than mine!

FRAZER. David. David don't take this the wrong way but there's this Bereavement Group –

DAVID. Thanks. No, really, thank you, I know you mean it kindly but –

FRAZER. It helped me a lot. Still does.

DAVID. But yes, as Christine was fond of saying, it wouldn't do if we were all the same.

FRAZER. See, it's a process –

DAVID. It's a fact. A fact I have to be getting on with.

I'm sorry, but if there is one thing that gives me the heebie-jeebies it's all this counselling crap and therapy-speak. Just not my cup of tea! At all.

See, I don't think there is anything wrong with me. If there is then I think that it's only right there's something wrong this stage of the game.

I miss her. What's wrong with that?

FRAZER. Will you take the number?

DAVID (*a beat, evenly*). Sure, if you tell me how much these books are.

FRAZER. Oh, I'll need to go and get Marjorie. She's the manageress, she does all the pricing.

DAVID. Frazer, don't disturb her, don't! I'll be back. I'll get them then. I'll need to do a clear out, I've plenty of books I'll never read again that I can bring over.

FRAZER. It's no bother. One second!

FRAZER exits backshop. DAVID looks at his watch. MARJORIE enters.

MARJORIE. Fifty pence! No! No, altogether!

She grabs the books, and shoves them in a bag for him.

DAVID. Take the quid. At least. I insist.

MARJORIE. Not at all –

DAVID. But there's a last year's *Halliwell's* and an as-new *Doctor Zhiva* –

MARJORIE. For goodness' sake, the amount of good things you brought in for us!

DAVID. And there's more! I'll bring them!

Exit DAVID. Just the moment he is gone, SUSAN appears with more things, and hangs them up.

MARJORIE. Charming man!

SUSAN (*automatically*). Really? Was he married?

Re-enter FRAZER. MARJORIE picks up the shoebox.

MARJORIE. What on earth is this? Oh my! Look at the make! They are an arm and a leg! You always see them with the Jimmy Choo's and the Manolo Thingy's in *Elle* and *Vogue* –

SUSAN takes the box from MARJORIE and she is the one to open it and, breathlessly, to take the beautiful shoes out of their tissue in the box. MARJORIE takes them.

Oh! Oh those are just gorgeous. They wouldn't even look at me with my high instep but they are just lovely!

Never been worn, look. Not a mark on the sole!

She puts them on the counter and, shaking her head at such profligacy, she exits backshop.

SUSAN. They're my size, but they look far too narrow.

FRAZER. Oh, try them on!

She does.

Oh my God. Do they fit?

She nods.

SUSAN. Like a glove.

SUSAN *dances and twirls about the place, smiling.*

FRAZER. Oh, Cinders, you shall go to the ball! Some day your prince will come! That is a gorgeous shoe! Not what you would call a wearing-shoe but very chic!

Hey Susan, buy them and wear them tonight for . . . you know! Hey, if you don't get a feller in lovely shoes like that with a pair of perfect pins like you've got, then I don't know what's wrong with men.

Re-enter MARJORIE.

MARJORIE. Off! You can't buy them! You know that! It's against the rules –

Shocked, SUSAN *takes them off.*

FRAZER. Marjorie, don't be so bloody stupid. Price them at your highest, I'll put in an extra fiver on top – we are not trying to cheat our charity, we're just trying to give Susan a treat.

MARJORIE. You know the rules and why they exist. For goodness' sake! With Joanne from Head Office due any moment!

MARJORIE *closes the box and, taking the shoes, she exits.*

SUSAN *can't speak. She is near tears. Walking away, almost comically upset, she waves her hands in front of her, as if to say 'Don't you say anything, especially anything nice to me.'*

FRAZER. She'll relent, Susan! Why does she have to be like that?

Winding herself up further, SUSAN shakes her head, tears about to spill, dumb-showing: 'Just keep away from me, Frazer, you're making it worse...'

They were so elegant! So *you*! You could've gone anywhere in those shoes. They would have given you confidence. Class. For a classy lady.

SUSAN wails: 'Please don't make it worse.' FRAZER has a rebellious thought which thrills him.

I'm going to put the wrong size on them or hide one till the six weeks are up and I'm allowed to buy you them. I will!

Enter DORIS from the changing room.

DORIS. Naw. No nothing! Tried oan the hale shoap but there was nothing suitable. Know thae days you lukk at yourself and you say I'm nicer in what I came in wi? Thanks.

She dumps a mess of clothes on counter, but, perversely, she returns a huge wedding hat to its proper place on a head in the window. She wheels round to reveal that the fitted coat she is wearing, and which looks, relatively, all right from the front, has two flaring contrast panel inserts in the back. She exits, but right at the door she wheels back in.

(*To SUSAN.*) Haw, whit is speed dating when it's at hame? Hope it's no whit I think it is!

Blackout.

End of Act One.

ACT TWO

FUNNY VALENTINE (*Comedy*)

Music: Jazzy instrumental of 'Love for Sale' (Cole Porter).

14 February. Before the audience's very eyes, in seconds, the shop is transformed to a place spectacularly decorated in red hearts for Valentine's Day.

As music fades, lights up on SUSAN and FRAZER. SUSAN, with dusters, Pledge and Windolene, is cleaning off and on throughout this exchange.

FRAZER is at the counter, sorting through a box of period textiles, embroidered cushion covers, etc.

SUSAN. I mean, what is the point?

FRAZER (*shrugs*). Search me, Susan.

SUSAN. Lying about your height? To somebody you're going to meet?

FRAZER finds a lovely, fifties-style, red-and-white-checked, frilly pinny and pops it on SUSAN, tying the strings behind her back to camp up her housework, and try to make her laugh. She lets him, but she's not to be deflected or distracted.

Lies. That's what you get, basically. OK, I've only done it three times and I've yet to get past the 'meet for a coffee' stage but what I'd say is it's often rubbish. Most people e-mail tripe about themselves, they really do.

They're all 'I run my own business' or 'financial services' or 'IT'. (*Sceptically.*) I'm sure!

(*Beat.*) I've seen some terrible toupees.

FRAZER. Is there any other sort?

SUSAN. Probably not. Last night's was a corker.

FRAZER. Last night's toupee?

SUSAN (*spelling it out*). No, last night's Internet Cupid's Connection.

FRAZER. What?

SUSAN. You heard me!

FRAZER. Look at what happened with that speed-dating carry-on.

SUSAN. That was then, this is now.

FRAZER. – And not content with that, now you've got to . . . go *online* and look for a 'cyber sweetheart'.

SUSAN. Frazer, get modern. Everybody does computer dating these days.

FRAZER. – Posting your intimate details on the web for all and sundry.

SUSAN. Anybody would think you didn't want me to find True Love and Happiness!

FRAZER. Darling, of course I do. It's just –

SUSAN. I know!

But it's not dangerous. You don't put down any details that could identify you, no addresses or anything, just first names, in fact your *nom de plume* –

FRAZER (*hands in the air*). Up to yourself!

SUSAN. Anyway, I was telling you about last night's Geek of the Week. Supposed to be forty-seven – uh-huh, and the rest! Former social worker suffering from burn-out, now a 'consultant'. 'Darkly handsome' – well, is that not for me to say, not him?

You'd think so.

He was . . . Swarthy, that's what I'd say. Sallow. Terrible blackheads, totally bald, broader than he was long but I thought to myself, 'Susan, you've got to stop judging by appearances – because I'm ashamed to say I do – the man's p'rhaps an interesting man, give him a chance', so I thought,

'OK, I'll meet him again, perhaps I'll go for a drink with him,' and he says to me he hopes I'm not offended but he won't ask to see me again because 'the spark is just there or it isn't' and he thinks it's better to be honest about these things, I'm a very nice lady but no spark.

FRAZER. I couldn't. I just couldn't. Imagine getting the thumbs-down from somebody you don't even fancy.

SUSAN. No. No, it didn't bother me to be quite honest. Rejection. When Tony left, yes. But a stranger? That I've never met before and I'll never meet again? (He said, 'Good luck with your quest!' Imagine! I nearly died!)

But I'm going to stick at all this carry-on and persevere because how else am I going to meet anyone? At my age?

FRAZER. Is that what you do? When you whatsit on the internet? Step it up from 'go for a coffee' to 'go for a drink'?

SUSAN. I think so. I'm hardly the expert but I think that's how it works. Meet in, say, Starbucks in somewhere impersonal, say, middle of town on late opening night, so if it doesn't work out – (Why should it work out? You do this stuff you take the long-term view, Frazer) – when it doesn't work out you can cut your losses and do a good freezer shop in Marks' and be back home before soap-time on the telly.

FRAZER. And if it works out?

SUSAN. If!

Well . . . I suppose next time you could meet for a drink? And if that worked out, following week you could arrange to go for a drink and a bite to eat. Perhaps swap phone numbers –

FRAZER. Oh my God, you better promise me you'll take good care of yourself! Because –

SUSAN. I'm hardly somebody some suave Casanova Conman's going to marry and murder for her money, am I?

FRAZER. You can't be too careful.

(Actually p'rhaps you can, I think that's been me all my life.)

But, oh, is it not kind of, I don't know – unnatural? Forced?

SUSAN. Like rhubarb?

FRAZER. No. Yes. I mean, you'll meet someone, Susan –

SUSAN. How? Where?

FRAZER. I honestly think you want to meet someone, you're meant to meet someone, you'll meet someone.

(Where does that leave me?)

SUSAN. There's no stigma nowadays. I'd even try that speed dating again.

FRAZER. Look where that got you!

SUSAN. He's got the message!

FRAZER. Eventually! Is that not a syndrome, that?

SUSAN. What?

FRAZER. De Somebody or Other's Syndrome. Being deluded that somebody's in love with you. I saw a programme about it on the telly: woman thought King George the Something was madly in love with her and sending her secret messages depending on how many curtains were drawn and how many not drawn on the front of Buckingham Palace.

SUSAN. He was harmless.

FRAZER. King George?

SUSAN. No, the guy that pestered me for a date, stupid!

The organiser of the speed dating told him she refused to forward any more correspondence to me and that was that.

FRAZER. – and there was a pair of identical twins both mad about some poor lorry driver whose life they made an absolute misery.

SUSAN. He was just a little bit persistent, that was all.

FRAZER. And the rest were all losers and weirdos as well; admit it.

SUSAN. Frazer, you want something, you've got to go for it. Take Positive Steps.

I'd do it again. And the internet. I'm even going to do an old-fashioned ad in that lonely hearts' column in the local rag. I'm not even particularly hopeful but I'll try.

FRAZER. GSOH?

SUSAN. What?

FRAZER. Good Sense of Humour.

SUSAN. Of course I have. I'll need it no doubt.

FRAZER. WLTM. You've got a good day for it, eh?

SUSAN. What? My birthday?

FRAZER. No, Valentine's! (*Dawns.*) Gosh –

SUSAN. – Forget it!

FRAZER. Oh, it is your birthday. I forgot! Some pal I am.

Valentine's Day! I knew that! You'd think I could've remembered –

SUSAN. It was perfect for Tony. He could kill two birds with one stone and forget Valentine's Day and my birthday in a one-er.

Ooh! My advert! Because I'm going to do one. Help me write it. Go on!

(*As she cleans.*) These mirrors! Who let in that mum with the sticky toddler?

SUSAN*'s housekeeping has taken her to the changing rooms.*

FRAZER. She wanted to try on a blouse.

SUSAN. And did she take it?

FRAZER. No . . .

SUSAN. Give me up the Windolene.

SUSAN *is inside the changing rooms now, behind the curtain. Pops back out again:*

– And the air freshener while you're at it!

She pops back in. During the following, SUSAN *keeps sticking her head out to chip in, then back inside again.* FRAZER *begins writing on a bit of paper.*

FRAZER. Attractive lady –

SUSAN. That means plain as a plate of chips but with a nice-enough nature.

FRAZER. Beautiful lady –

SUSAN. Hey! Steady on. Trade Descriptions Act.

FRAZER. Lovely lady. That's more like it? Strike a balance. Lovely lady (you are though)! Late forties –

SUSAN *and* FRAZER (*in unison*). Forty-something!

SUSAN *pops head back inside and now stays in.*

FRAZER. Young-looking, young-acting forty-something WLTM.

MARJORIE *appears from backshop. Caught by what* FRAZER, *apparently alone, is saying and doing, she stands at the door, quietly listening.*

Would like to meet . . . Man. Mature. Genuine. Caring. GSOH. Faithful. No, loyal. (Loyal's lovely.) Sensitive. A man . . . In touch with his feminine side. Own hair and teeth. OHAT.

For . . .

Fun. Companionship. Maybe more. Long winter afternoons curled up watching old black-and-whites on the telly.

MARJORIE *comes right out and touches his shoulder.*

MARJORIE. – Oh, Frazer, that's lovely!

FRAZER. What?

MARJORIE. I think it's so lovely that you've decided to . . . to 'come out of the closet', is that what they say? At your age. And look for love. And why not?

I'm not shocked, Frazer.

I think you'll find it's a changed climate generally.

People are broad-minded. These days. But I still think you're very brave.

(*Confiding.*) If you don't mind me saying so, I'm not actually totally one hundred per cent surprised.

FRAZER. Marjorie, it's not –

MARJORIE. Well, it won't be! Tea's up through the back, pet. Come through, yeah? And we can 'talk'.

If you want to . . .

MARJORIE *exits backshop.* SUSAN *comes out in hysterics of laughter.*

FRAZER. I know who should've come out the closet!

SUSAN. Oh Frazer, darling, I couldn't. I really, really don't want Marjorie's sympathy. Or her help. Christ, no.

FRAZER. But she thinks –

SUSAN. Let her. For me. Go on.

FRAZER. Ooh . . . *You!* What would I not do for you!

Smiling, SUSAN *picks up the ad copy, reads and sighs.*

FRAZER *covers up his (perhaps) over-fondness for* SUSAN *by camping it up, making light of his worry.*

Hey, Suze!

See once you've hooked your dream lover, what about our salsa nights, eh? Will you still chum me on a Tuesday?

SUSAN. Damn tootin'! (*Beat.*) Oh, I'll never meet anyone anyway.

FRAZER. Why not? Susan, you've got so much to offer.

SUSAN. Oh, I know that. My self-esteem hasn't slipped that low. I do have a lot to offer and of course I'm not about to offer it to just anyone.

'member that Stones' song? 'Ti-i-i-ime is on my side, yes it is . . . '?

'*Not*' – as Stephi would say.

Bloke my age with his own hair and teeth – no, strike the condition. Too stringent.

Bloke my age with a pulse, he can start over dead easy, find himself some fresh young bit and begin again.

Was reading an article in the *GQ* there. At the dentist. And it was perfectly brazen about it, it had a little formula about Every Man's Ideal Age for a Girlfriend or Partner and it went like this: Half Your Age Plus Seven. So . . . it works. It does.

Try it out. OK . . . Marjorie's big son Steven, what age is he? Sixteen. Half his age that's eight, plus seven that's fifteen, I'm sure that'd do him very nicely, thank you.

And take Tony. Take my husband. Please . . .

(And she certainly did.)

Well, Tony's fifty, half that is twenty-five plus seven that's thirty-two. I believe the Dreaded Natalie is a youngish thirty-something . . . ? No doubt with tits out to here, I wouldn't know. I'm yet to clap eyes on the bitch, anyway, anyway . . .

Now, I'm forty-nine, do the sum backwards. So take away seven, that's forty-two, double it. I'm the ideal age of girlfriend for a man of eighty-four. Which is Dad's age.

And I'm living with my Old Dad so there's got to be an irony there somewhere.

Enter DORIS *in the same coat and tea-cosy hat as before.*

DORIS. Did yous get a Valentine? Neither did Ah.

They acknowledge her: an exhausted wave from SUSAN, *a flamboyant ironic bow from* FRAZER. DORIS *begins to browse.*

SUSAN. Do you know, I don't really blame men, Frazer.

FRAZER. Oh, I do!

SUSAN. If I'm in the street and I see some attractive man, invariably I think about it, he'll be . . . oh, late thirties maximum, and certainly not about to be interested in me!

My 'Oh, He's Nice!' meter is stuck way back in the era I used to be using it last!

I don't think I fancy men over forty, frankly.

FRAZER. Some of us are OK, surely?

DORIS *has found something, and shows it to* SUSAN.

DORIS. Here, that's nice. What would you say that shade was?

SUSAN. Lovatt?

DORIS. Aye, so do I, but what would you cry it? Sortae sage? Kinna dark odeneel, intit? Between that and a sortae pale greenish donkey.

The phone rings and SUSAN *answers it.* DORIS *gathers a garment or two, eavesdropping.*

SUSAN. Speaking. (*Listens.*) Oh. (*Listens.*) Oh dear. (*Listens.*) Without his trous . . . ? (*Listens.*) Oh dear. (*Listens.*) Oh dear. Yes, I can see that. (*Listens.*) No, he's never done that before. (*Listens.*) No, I'll come over the road. I'll come home, it's no bother, be right there.

She hangs up.

The home help. Little bit of a domestic emergency. With Dad. I'll have to pop home, I'm sure I'll be right back –

SUSAN *exits backshop.*

DORIS. Can I try them?

FRAZER. You know where to go, Doris.

DORIS *disappears into the changing room as* SUSAN *rushes out from backshop with her coat flung on. Grabbing her bag,* SUSAN *exits by the front door, bumping hard into* DAVID *who is carrying a big cardboard box before him. He drops the box.*

DAVID. Sorry! (*Meaning: 'Manners! Can't you apologise too?'*)

FRAZER. Hello! Back again! David, isn't it?

DAVID *dumps the box on the counter. A couple of sad suits still in hangers are sticking out. He grabs a bag off the top and grabs a handful of ties from inside it, spilling them onto the counter –*

DAVID. Ties! Who needs them?

– in a not-very-brightly-coloured silken heap of mainly striped and rather conservative numbers.

I mean, what a stupid appendage! One little strip of cloth to express ourselves.

And women have all this! Rainbows! Herbaceous borders –

He indicates the rows of dresses. MARJORIE *enters, and stands in the doorway, listening, concerned.*

FRAZER. Oh, I know! I often envy women their clothes, don't you?

DAVID. Well . . . I wouldn't say that, but –

MARJORIE. Frazer –

FRAZER. You are looking so fine. There is something different about you since the last time you were in here –

DAVID. Big clear-out! Psychologically good for you, don't they say? None of the young guys at work would be seen dead with a tie on. And these suits! What an old sad-sack I've been going to work, it's unnecessary.

FRAZER. Do you remember David, Marjorie? Isn't he looking great?

MARJORIE. Frazer –

DAVID. Dumping the whole damn lot of them, 'cept kept the bow tie for my dinner jacket and the black one for funerals.

FRAZER. And we hope, David, it'll be a long long while before either you or me's got another one of them.

MARJORIE. Oh, absolutely –

FRAZER. Looking fine! You really are.

DAVID. Thanks a lot! Emm . . . You're looking fit yourself . . .

MARJORIE. Frazer –

DAVID. I sort of took myself in hand, I thought Christine'd have been the first to remind me that life's for the living –

FRAZER. Oh, so it is, you should try new things! Speaking of . . . Tell me . . . Did you ring That Number . . . ?

MARJORIE. Frazer –

FRAZER (*mouthing*). 'member? That number I suggested –

MARJORIE. Frazer! There's a beautiful little cashmere cardie come in but it unfortunately needs debobbling, it's in urgent need of your services. Through the back.

FRAZER. Marjorie, I'm just having a little chat with –

MARJORIE. Yes, I do know David –

FRAZER. Can't it wait?

MARJORIE. You're our ultimate defuzzer, Frazer, as well you know!

FRAZER. Marjorie –

MARJORIE. Can I just have a little moment here, please, Frazer!

What can he say? FRAZER *exits backshop.* MARJORIE *makes a beeline for* DAVID *and touches his arm.*

(*Very confidentially.*) I hope he's not coming on too strong, David.

DAVID. No, not at all, Marjorie. I can call you Marjorie, can I? You don't mind me calling you by your first name? Because I don't think we've actually been formally introduced.

If she's being (nicely and subtly) rebuked it's wasted on her.

MARJORIE (*grandly*). Feel free, David, of course. It's just that I was concerned that he . . . Bit much? Eh?

DAVID. He's only got my interests at heart, Marjorie.

MARJORIE. Well, if you –

DAVID. He means well.

MARJORIE. That's very –

DAVID. Of course, I'm not that way inclined myself.

MARJORIE. I didn't think so.

DAVID. I'm not, and he knows that. I said, 'Not my cup of tea, no, sorry!'

But it's not as if he's the type to ram it down your throat, is he?

MARJORIE. I hope not.

DAVID. I was absolutely straight with him, and that was no problem. I think he preferred it.

But see, Marjorie, I look at it this way: it's very kind of him, I mean, from his point of view if something does something for you, well, obviously you can't help being . . . what? That little bit messianic about it? Can you? It's only natural.

MARJORIE. I'm glad you look at it that way.

DAVID. I do.

MARJORIE. Because I was worried in case . . .

DAVID. I can see that, but no need on my behalf, I can assure you.

MARJORIE. Because you see it's very very recent . . .

DAVID. Really? Oh, I thought it was a little while . . .

MARJORIE. Well, as far as him acknowledging it. Openly.

DAVID. So it was hard for him to accept it?

MARJORIE. Oh yes, oh, I think so, and of course denial . . .

DAVID. Touch of the Anthony Perkins's, eh?

MARJORIE. I don't follow . . .

DAVID *makes stabbing motions and imitates the* Psycho *soundtrack as her bafflement increases.*

DAVID. Ee! Ee! Ee! Ee! Bates Motel – Sorry, Marjorie, that was a sick joke and the last thing I'd ever want to do is make a fool of Frazer's feelings. (Coughs.) Sorry . . . Sorry?

No, no, I understand, that makes things a lot clearer. He was in denial. I see. I see . . . That'll be why the telephone thing'll have been somewhat of a lifeline for him?

MARJORIE. You're very tolerant.

DAVID. Of course!

MARJORIE. I'm glad to say!

DAVID. Well, the way I see it is everybody deals with these things in very different ways. Some folk like to get together in big touchy-feely groups, others – like me – are just more inclined to grin and bear it, just sort of stick it out in private.

MARJORIE *gives him a look –*

MARJORIE. Right . . .

– and exits backshop, sharpish. As DAVID *makes for the door,* SUSAN*'s father* ARCHIE, *an old man of eighty-four, somewhat bewildered, enters and grabs him by the sleeve.*

ARCHIE. . . . Where's our Susan? Somebody said to me I'll find our Susan in here.

DAVID. Sorry, I'm not –

ARCHIE. . . . What are all these clothes doing in Fullerton the Ironmongers'? Where's Jack Fullerton?

DAVID. Mr Dickinson, it's you, isn't it?

ARCHIE. . . . Yes, Archibald Dickinson, that's me, do I know your face? You're familiar . . . but to tell you the truth, I've been diagnosed with a little bit of memory loss.

DAVID. I know you. You're Mr Dickinson the plumber. You put in a bathroom for us but you'll not remember that, why should you?

ARCHIE. . . . I do a lot of bathrooms. How's your wife?

DAVID. I'm afraid my wife died.

ARCHIE. . . . Oh, I'm sorry to hear that.

DAVID. Made a lovely job of our bathroom, you did!

ARCHIE. . . . Do you know, I think I came out the house there for a pound and a half of mince for the wife but I can't find Gardeners the Butchers'.

DAVID. Ah well . . .

ARCHIE. . . . Because our Susan's supposed to be coming up tonight with her Spanish boyfriend so of course she's wanting to make them Spaghetti Bolognese . . .

DAVID. Aaah . . . Frazer! Frazer! Marjorie!

Enter MARJORIE *from backshop.*

MARJORIE. He's away out the back at the bins, David, it's collection day. (*Shouting as if to a deaf person.*) Mr Dickinson, what are you doing here, I thought Susan was away home looking for you?

ARCHIE (*shouting back*). What is she looking for me for, because I'm normally at my work?

MARJORIE (*confidentially to* DAVID, *shaking head*). Confused.

Well, just you sit there for a minute, Mr Dickinson. I'm sure she'll be back in just a little minute.

ARCHIE. . . . No, I can't stop because I'm to get something or other for the wife. Wonder what it was . . .

MARJORIE (*confidentially to* DAVID, *shaking head*). Dead. Years ago!

Mr Dickinson, why don't you go through the back with David here and sit and have yourself a little cup of tea?

ARCHIE. . . . Because I'm getting forgetful, you know. To tell the truth, I've been diagnosed with a little bit of memory loss.

MARJORIE (*confidentially to* DAVID, *shaking head*). Tragic!

That's a good idea, come on through here with David . . .

ARCHIE (*to* DAVID). Who are you? Any relation of Jack Fullerton?

How's your wife? Is she keeping OK?

DAVID *manoeuvres* ARCHIE *backshop as* MARJORIE *looks out of the window.*

MARJORIE. Och Susan! Susan, where are you, for goodness' sake . . . No sign . . . I wonder if she's got her mobile?

MARJORIE *dials the phone.*

Susan, there you are! Where are you? Your dad's here! (*Listens.*) Mmm. Mmm. No, he's fine. Well, a little bit confused for sure, but he's fine, we've got him having a little cuppa through the back with Frazer and David. (*Listens.*) You know David! You do!

Oh, never mind, your dad's just dandy! OK, OK, see you in a little minute. Susan, don't rush, he's perfectly all right.

DAVID *returns from backshop.*

DAVID. I'm just off. Frazer seems to be having a job finding the Empire Biscuits he's promised Mr Dickinson.

MARJORIE *rolls her eyes at the incompetence she puts up with.*

MARJORIE. I can't tempt you?

MARJORIE *exits backshop. Grinning,* DAVID *nods his goodbye, but he is beaten to his exit by a muffled* DELIVERY MAN *who enters with big bunch of red roses and a heart card, blocking him.*

DELIVERY MAN. I'll need a signature, please.

DAVID. Can't help you, pal, sorry, I don't work here.

DAVID *tries again for the door, but the* DELIVERY MAN *stops him.*

DELIVERY MAN. Flowers for Love, it's a same-day delivery. Just sign for them.

DAVID. Frazer! Marjorie!

MARJORIE *comes back out.*

MARJORIE. Oh my! These are beautiful!

Wait there just one little second, David, please, could you? (*Signs chit and reads card.*) Seems our Susan must have a secret admirer! Well, well, there's a turn-up for the books.

The DELIVERY MAN *exits.*

David, I meant to ask you, you couldn't do me a favour and bring that box of yours – (it was awfully good of you) – through the back for me, only, poor old Frazer's disc's playing up again and the consultant was adamant I'm not supposed to do any heavy lifting for a full year after my little op.

DAVID. Of course.

Ushered by MARJORIE, DAVID *begins to lift the box and bring it through the back. Leaving the plastic bag with the spilling bundle of ties on the counter.*

MARJORIE. Course it was keyhole and quite frankly, a couple of weeks later there was damn all wrong with me.

What on earth have you been bringing us? Books! They're so blinking heavy, aren't they –

DAVID. Books, CDs, videos, two fondue sets . . .

MARJORIE. Oh absolutely!

They exit backshop just as SUSAN *comes in through the front door and, on her way towards the back, does a double take, arrested by the sight of the roses.*

SUSAN. Oh my! Somebody loves somebody.

She looks at the card. And backs off as if it's radioactive.

Is somebody taking the piss? Frazer! Frazer!

FRAZER *sticks his head out from backshop.*

FRAZER. Hi there, Susan, the old fella's fine. Wants to put a new washer on our tap. That'll be him for hours, eh? Happy as Larry . . .

SUSAN *is still examining the roses, amazed. Behind* SUSAN, DAVID *comes out from backshop, dusting his hands.*

Hearing his footsteps, SUSAN, *thinking it's* FRAZER, *turns and hugs him.*

SUSAN. Did you send these? Frazer, you're –

DAVID. Not guilty, no. Flowers for Love, that's what the man said!

SUSAN. Oh! Sorry, sorry, I thought you were . . . Excuse me!

SUSAN, *covered in confusion, flees backshop, dropping the bouquet.* FRAZER *enters from backshop crossing with her.* DAVID *picks up the roses from the floor.*

DAVID. These don't seem to have had the desired effect . . .

FRAZER. You sent roses . . . ?

DAVID. No. Why'd I send anybody roses? I just meant,
somebody –

FRAZER *is reading the card.*

FRAZER. Sent roses to Susan? 'All My Love from You Know
Who . . . '? You'd think she'd be pleased . . .

DAVID. My point entirely.

FRAZER. Anyway, David, as I was trying to ask you earlier
before I got so rudely interrupted – (Marjorie, honest to
God, what is she on?) – how are you? In yourself.

DAVID. I'm fine. Most of the time. I'm sleeping better. I seem
to accept now that Christine's gone. I still miss her. Always
will, no question about that, but . . . Things've changed. The
house feels different now. Don't laugh – perhaps you'll
know what I'm talking about? – but for months and months
I'd go into a room and I'd feel she'd just left. Not her
perfume exactly – and there was nothing spooky about this
feeling, quite the reverse, it was a comfort if anything. Her
presence, you know? Often as if she was in the house but in
another room. I mean, I knew it was just in my imagination
but it felt quite real to me and . . . Recently it's changed.
She's gone.

FRAZER. Oh, I know what you mean, sometimes when I go in
that door I'm just expecting my old mum to be sat there in
that kitchen!

DAVID. No, what I'm saying, I *don't* –

FRAZER. No, I know exactly what you mean!

DAVID. The worse thing I can do to Christine's memory is try
and turn her into some kind of saint. 'Cos she sure wasn't.
Neither of us were! We made a lot of mistakes, had a lot of
ups and downs like anybody else, two or three bad patches
where I tell you it was touch and go if we made it as a
couple . . . but we had the boys, and we got through it.
Somehow. (*Smiles.*) And the last four or five years, before

she was diagnosed, yes, and after it too – well, that is often the way of it, is it not?

FRAZER. I don't think I'll ever get over my mother!

DAVID. No, no, I can see that. (*Beat.*) Have you redecorated?

FRAZER. Eh? I'm changing things around. Got rid of the television. Phoned up the Salvation Army and they came up and took it off my hands. I don't miss it, not one bit. I've been reading a lot and listening to music, I used to be a big jazz buff, you know, but some of those LPs I've not listened to for years.

I've tried taking myself out to the movies, but –

Anyway, life moves on. New beginnings. I can't help but feel that something is about to happen. Well . . . for instance –

Through the door comes a youngish thirty-something woman, festooned with expensive carriers from Scandalrags boutique. This (and, though we may well suspect, we are yet to know it) is NATALIE.

NATALIE. Excuse me, can I try that shoe in the window?

FRAZER. Surely.

FRAZER *remembers the provenance of the shoe and wishes to protect* DAVID.

FRAZER. Is that you off, David?

NATALIE. It's the one on the heart-shaped cushion, I'm sure it's a –

FRAZER. Yes, it is! I know just the shoe you're talking about, only –

NATALIE. Can I try it?

FRAZER. Surely.

FRAZER *reluctantly goes to window, brings it back to her.*

NATALIE. I think it says . . . Am I right, is it a thirty-seven? Oh, right foot, is it?

FRAZER. It is, but . . .

NATALIE. That's my size normally. It's brand new! Oh gosh, oh gosh, that is just perfect, isn't it? What do you think?

She tries the shoe on and stretches out her leg like Anne Bancroft in The Graduate, *skirt above knee, right at* DAVID *who, of course, recognises the shoe. He is affected by a sudden pang of grief.*

DAVID. Oh! Oh, very nice, I'm sure. Excuse me.

DAVID *exits.*

NATALIE. What's the matter with your other assistant? Did I offend him?

FRAZER. No. No. He doesn't work here, no, just a little . . . emotional moment there, I suspect.

For emotional reasons.

NATALIE *is puzzled, but much more interested in swivelling her ankle and admiring her own shapely leg in the lovely shoe.*

NATALIE. Right . . . Can I try the other foot?

FRAZER. The left?

NATALIE. Yeah, right.

FRAZER. No, that's the thing, I'm sorry. We've only got the one.

NATALIE. The what?

FRAZER. The one.

NATALIE. The one?

FRAZER. Uh-huh.

NATALIE. Of the pair?

FRAZER. Uh-huh. I assume. If they were a pair.

NATALIE. Really? Surely –

FRAZER. Well, we've mislaid it, obviously. Or else it came in like that.

NATALIE. The one shoe?

FRAZER. Or it was stolen.

NATALIE. One shoe? Somebody . . . ?

FRAZER. Well, the other's here, so . . .

SUSAN *enters, waving her book.*

SUSAN. I don't believe it. My *Doctor Zhivago* that I lost! (I take it all back, Marjorie! I was sure she'd sold it because she so very vehemently denied it.)

SUSAN *sees* NATALIE *wearing 'her' shoe.*

Oh, sorry! Oh! Somebody's found a bargain!

SUSAN *and* FRAZER *are quite complicit throughout the following. It's not the first time they've pulled this stunt. SUSAN is slightly shocked at herself, which makes her enjoy it even more; she's quite near the giggles throughout.*

NATALIE. Well, I thought so, only –

SUSAN. *Don't* tell me it's still not turned up, Frazer?

FRAZER. Neither hide nor hair of it unfortunately.

SUSAN. Really?

FRAZER. And do you know, I'm beginning to think it never will.

NATALIE. You're joking! Oh well, I should have known I wasn't the get-a-great-bargain-in-a-charity-shop type! Girl in my office kits herself out constantly from top to toe in secondhand shops and looks a million dollars.

SUSAN. I know, some people just seem to have an eye, don't they? And the knack.

NATALIE. – She got a Nicole Farhi in the Marie Curie!

SUSAN. Oh, it wouldn't be me!

NATALIE. – She *says.* Yeah, right! Because of course it's nothing but a reverse sort of one-upmanship, if you ask me.

You know: 'I got that exact Versace jacket in Oxfam.'

'Paid full price for your Prada bag, did you? You're a mug, 'cos I got mine in TK Maxx for a fiver.'

(*Beat.*) Basically, you want to kill the cow.

FRAZER. Is the one no good to you?

NATALIE. Eh?

FRAZER. Because it'd just be the half price, obviously . . .

NATALIE. Pardon?

SUSAN. Frazer!

FRAZER. What? Well, somebody's going to want it . . .

With a theatrical sigh he replaces the shoe in the window, then goes to the counter and picks up the roses.

NATALIE. Look, if you would just take a look –

FRAZER. I'll take these through –

NATALIE. Please! OK?

FRAZER. – and I'll put them in water because if you ask me, somebody round here is very ungrateful indeed!

SUSAN. Frazer, I'm –

But he's off through the back. To herself, though NATALIE *overhears:*

Shouldn't have, he really shouldn't . . .

NATALIE. Little crush on you, has he? You can't tell can you, like my hairdresser, you'd totally swear he was camp as Chloë but, no, as you were, he's happily married with three kids!

SUSAN. My someone's been splashing out today already! Scandalrags, eh, lucky you, I always look in their window and wish.

NATALIE. You should go in!

SUSAN. They're beyond my budget and that's for sure!

NATALIE. No, you get to your age, you need a bit of class in the clothes department. Look at this . . .

She drags out a simple but classy top from one carrier bag, and holds it up.

See, this would suit you. Because you've got a lovely figure.

SUSAN. Me!

NATALIE. Oh, you have. For your age, stunning!

As the woman said to me: 'With perhaps a plain pant?' And it wasn't dear.

She shows SUSAN *the price tag.* SUSAN *grimaces in unfeigned shock.*

Not for what it is.

SUSAN. If you say so!

It's lovely all the same! Special occasion coming up?

NATALIE. No, not really. It's not that! Just fancied it.

SUSAN. Indulge yourself!

NATALIE. Why not?

SUSAN. Nobody else is going to!

NATALIE. Well . . . Ajay indulges me all the time actually, but I've got to not leave it up to him to do the choosing. Men, eh? They'd have you running around in raunchy, red-lace, see-through bra-and-thong sets – oh, which you've to wear below butter-wouldn't-melt, duck-egg-blue, retro, angora twinsets that make you look like a cross between Nigella Lawson and the first teacher they ever adored in the mixed infants!

I go, 'Ajay, thank you, but exactly *who* is this a present *for*?'

NATALIE *catches sight of the heart-patterned tie sticking out of the top of* DAVID's *bag, and pulls it out like a lovely silken snake.*

Oh, hearts, look! I'm sure it's silk! My, that'd be a lovely little Valentine's Day extra.

SUSAN. Does he wear ties?

Because men don't much these days, do they? Mine never –

NATALIE. No?

SUSAN. Not really.

NATALIE. Oh, Ajay really likes to get dressed up.

SUSAN. Lucky you. Mine was a slob.

NATALIE. When we go out. Like tonight he's insisting we go
out for dinner. Well, it's not that it's Valentine's Day as
such; it's more that it's our anniversary, two years to the day
since we actually . . . you know! For the first time.

Course I'd fancied him for absolutely ages!

(*Of tie.*) I have to get this. I really do!

Tell you, tonight quite frankly I'd as soon stay home.
Honestly. Heartburn. It's really shocking. I'm nearly two
months pregnant and nobody told me that morning sickness
was more like morning, noon and night!

I'm getting married in a month's time too. I hope to God it's
stopped by then or I'll not be the bonny blushing bride, I'll
be the pale green and permanently puking bride!

Course he's over the moon; well, men always are, aren't
they? They just love pregnant women.

SUSAN. Mine didn't.

NATALIE. No?

SUSAN. Not really.

NATALIE. Ajay's signing up for the breathing classes, the lot.

SUSAN. I suppose it's not actually his fault. I went into
labour a month early and he was in Barcelona at the big
match while I was getting an emergency Caesarean – but
oh well . . . He's always been a great dad, I'll give him that.
Once our daughter was born, he enjoyed that. We both did.
When she was little . . .

NATALIE. How old is she now?

SUSAN. Fifteen.

NATALIE. Oh, don't! My step-daughter's fifteen! Great lump,
so she is, that Stephanie. Ajay says, 'Natalie, there's no
need to put up with cheek from her, she knows I won't
tolerate it.'

SUSAN (*reeling*). Excuse me, it's just occurred to me I think I might know where that shoe is.

SUSAN *exits backshop. NATALIE looks around puzzled. Then she holds out, and rolls up the tie, savouring it.*

NATALIE. Gorgeous . . .

SUSAN *steams back on with the shoebox containing the left shoe wrapped in tissue. FRAZER comes running on after her.*

SUSAN. Here it is!

NATALIE. Gosh! I'm in luck then.

SUSAN. Looks like it!

FRAZER. What are you doing? I think you'll find, I think you'll find the heel's broken! You can't sell that shoe, it's dangerous!

NATALIE. Nonsense, it looks absolutely fine! Give me a little shot of the other one again.

FRAZER. They're very expensive.

NATALIE. Not at all! Because they're normally extortionate!

SUSAN. Frazer! You must have them! Of course you must.

NATALIE *puts them on, and kicks her heels in pleasure.*

NATALIE. Oh yes! Yes! YES! They are divine!

SUSAN. Take them!

NATALIE *stands and sashays across the room in them.*

FRAZER. For God's sake!

She twirls, then stops, takes a dithering beat or two.

NATALIE. . . . But you know, the left one does pinch a little bit . . .

SUSAN. It'll stretch!

NATALIE. Maybe . . . (*Beat. Walks again. Considers.*) I'm not sure it will.

FRAZER. It's a mistake to buy a shoe that doesn't fit you perfectly!

NATALIE. I know. I know, but I just –

FRAZER. Big mistake. Bunions before you –

NATALIE. God forbid. But they are *so* lovely . . .

FRAZER. But they don't fit you!

NATALIE (*long beat*). You're right. You're right. It is so, so weird too because normally my left foot is slightly smaller than the right, I can't understand it.

She takes them off, shaking her head in disappointment.
FRAZER *grabs them.*

FRAZER. There you go! You made the right decision.

NATALIE. I'll take that tie though.

FRAZER. This? It's not priced.

NATALIE. How much do they normally go for?

SUSAN. £1.99. Invariably.

FRAZER. Or more!

NATALIE. It's immaculate! I'd have paid a tenner.

SUSAN. Done!

FRAZER. But it's not priced!

SUSAN. Well, I've sold it! Ten quid to you!

NATALIE. Gosh, I don't actually have any cash! Do you take credit cards, I don't suppose so . . .

SUSAN. Or cheque!

NATALIE. Well, great! (*Begins writing a cheque.*) Ooh! He'll love it! He'll just so so love it!

SUSAN. Good!

NATALIE. Do you want my card? Will I put the number?

SUSAN. No, it's fine, I'm sure we can trust you.

NATALIE. You sure?

NATALIE *exits with the tie, but without the shoes. As she goes:*

Oh, do you know, I could just spit about those shoes!

FRAZER. That was a close thing!

Ruby slippers! Talk about lucky! I'm buying you them, I am, as a belated birthday present next week once they've survived Marjorie's six-weeks-on-sale-before-staff-eligible-to-purchase rule.

SUSAN. I don't want them.

FRAZER. What's the matter?

SUSAN. That was Natalie.

FRAZER. You mean . . .

SUSAN. Natalie. Antony James's, sorry, Ajay's, new little . . .

She waves the signed cheque in front of his face, then puts it in the till.

FRAZER. Her? No! She's practically young enough to be his –

SUSAN. – girlfriend. Yes. Exactly.

FRAZER. Well, at least she never got your shoes!

SUSAN. She might as well have, she's got everything else. Go on! Take my husband, buy my daughter's affection by giving her everything money can buy, letting her do everything that Bad Old Mum won't let her do because she's too young, give her the thrill of being a Big Sister . . .

FRAZER. You mean she's –

SUSAN. Yup!

FRAZER. Well, I suppose it was on the cards.

SUSAN. Yup!

FRAZER. You had already come up with that particular 'someday' scenario yourself.

SUSAN. Yup. Stephi will be thrilled!

FRAZER. Susan, you said your Stephi couldn't stand the Dreaded Natalie –

An enormous and horrible realisation hits SUSAN: *'What a bastard!'*

SUSAN. Oh my God!

FRAZER. What?

SUSAN. Huh! Now I know where Tony was and exactly what he was up to on my forty-seventh birthday!

FRAZER. You said to me things between you and Tony were dead long before –

SUSAN. OK! OK!

FRAZER. You'd nothing in common really except Stephi, you never had sex except once in a blue moon –

SUSAN. I know, I know.

FRAZER. – 'A very very blue moon, with the lights out and over in no time and personally you'd have preferred a cup of tea.' These are your own exact words. I'm quoting.

SUSAN. I don't think that's uncommon, Frazer, not after twenty odd years!

FRAZER. Well, perhaps not, what would I know, nothing, I've never been married and the way you describe you and Tony, well, if that's typical, I can't say I've missed much. I know one thing, my mother never felt like that about my dad. Adored him. When he died she couldn't begin to cope without him –

SUSAN. Frazer, it's one thing going along as usual, living quite the thing in a flatline marriage with a fairly friendly semi-stranger, and another being all of a sudden dumped and having to witness your husband be far from flatline with a girl half his age.

FRAZER. Plus seven!

SUSAN. Oh shut up, you!

DORIS's *hand comes through curtain, holding out some garments.*

DORIS (*off*). No, these are definite no-nos, you can hing them back up. I've a couple of mibbes, but.

SUSAN *goes and takes them.*

SUSAN. Lovatt not do it for you? Just you take your time,
Doris . . .

A thought planted by NATALIE *crosses* SUSAN's *mind.*

Frazer. Frazer, listen, darling, you did send me these roses
for my birthday, didn't you, not for Valentine's?

FRAZER. Me? I never sent you the roses at all, Susan.

SUSAN. Then who did?

FRAZER *shrugs and holds up the 'ruby slippers', plays
with them, puts them on his hands to wear and points them
at* SUSAN *throughout the following.*

FRAZER. Ooh! Absolutely no bloody thanks to you they're
still here, madam! My heart was in my mouth there. I
could've brained you! 'Positive Steps'? 'Positive Steps'?
You've got a real streak of negativity, you have.

SUSAN. Me?

FRAZER. Because you do deserve these (*Of the shoes.*) and
there are attractive, available men out there. Without you
resorting to desperate measures.

SUSAN. There is nothing desperate about me, Frazer, if I
manage to meet someone on the internet or via the lonely
hearts' column or however so be it. If not, I'll live. I would
like to, I'd like for that whole side of my life not to be
totally over, but I'm really not banking on it.

MARJORIE *comes swanning out from backshop, carrying*
SUSAN's *flowers in a vase* –

MARJORIE. Say what you like about similar demographics,
but the stuff they sent over from the other branch isn't a
patch on what we sent them.

– *which she puts on the counter with a flourish.*

My, Susan, you're a dark horse!

Flustered, FRAZER *catches himself with the shoes in his
hands, so pushes them deep into* DAVID's *bag with the ties
on top to hide them.*

FRAZER. Oh, err, I was just saying to Susan that there are attractive, unattached, available men you can meet, eh, Marjorie? Even in middle age. I mean, take me, take David.

SUSAN. Who's David?

FRAZER. David! You saw him, he's a widower, he's –

MARJORIE. – In a relationship, Frazer, sorry to disappoint you!

FRAZER. Eh? David? I don't think so, Marjorie, he certainly never gave me that impression.

MARJORIE. Well, I'm sorry, but he's got a girlfriend.

FRAZER. Has he?

SUSAN. Of course he has! (Whoever he is . . .)

MARJORIE. Oh yes. He made that very clear to me in our little chat. The first thing he made he told me! He's a normal heterosexual male, Frazer . . .

SUSAN. . . . And your normal heterosexual male doesn't lack female company for very long! Widower? Do you know how long the average widower goes before he has another relationship?

FRAZER. No, but –

SUSAN. How long?

FRAZER. Oh . . . A couple of years? I dunno, but –

SUSAN. Six months! And how long for the average widow?

FRAZER. I don't know. Longer. Presumably. Three years?

SUSAN. Thirteen. Widowers, six months. Widows, thirteen years. On average.

FRAZER. You're hell of a keen on numbers and statistics these days, Susan. (This that bloody magazine at the dentist again?) I mean, people are people, they don't necessarily fit into statistics.

MARJORIE. Nor do leopards change their spots, Fraze. Just think about it, pet, please, for your own sake.

FRAZER. Eh?

MARJORIE. Because I wouldn't like to see you getting hurt, that's all.

SUSAN (*looking out of the window*). Oh my God, there's that guy, that I . . . He's coming in! I'm away –

DAVID enters, just in time to see the very back of SUSAN *as she flees.*

FRAZER. David! Back again!

DAVID. I am. Thing is . . . This is embarrassing, but I brought over something I shouldn't have. Can I take a look?

MARJORIE. Of course! If you just brought it over, David, it'll be still there. Nothing's even priced yet. Can I help you? What exactly is it?

DAVID. Oh, it's OK, Marjorie. It's just a . . . it was a present in fact, a tie, and I should never –

FRAZER. Were there hearts on it?

DAVID. Yes.

FRAZER. (I knew it . . .)

MARJORIE. Well, it'll still be there. Definitely. Hearts?

She begins to look with him.

On a tie? In a pattern kind of thing? (*Shouting.*) Susan! Did you see David's tie? Susan! Come here!

MARJORIE, *in her rummaging, finds the ruby slippers deep in the bag. She stands them up, in all their glory, on the counter.*

Well, would you credit it! The pair! Because, David, I know these were a kind donation from you and I tell you we could have sold them ten times over in the past few weeks only there was only ever the one of them could be found, it was a total mystery! (*Shouting.*) Susan! Susan, you definitely never sold a heart-patterned tie of David's, did you?

FRAZER. But they weren't even priced yet, Marjorie!

MARJORIE. I know! You sure you brought it over, David?

DAVID. Yes, I'm afraid that I did.

MARJORIE. I'll away through and see if by any chance it fell in the box with those books of yours, David!

MARJORIE exits backshop. DAVID keeps looking, delving to the bottom of the bag, ever more worried. The phone rings. FRAZER answers.

FRAZER. Hello. (*Beat.*) Yes, it is, yes! (*Beat.*) Yes, she is. (*Calls.*) Susan, it's for you. SUSAN! PHONE!

Reluctantly, SUSAN enters and takes the phone. FRAZER takes DAVID aside.

SUSAN (*phone*). Hello, hello, who is this? (*Listens.*) Excuse me? (*Listens.*) No, no, I did not send a Valentine message to you, you're dreaming.

DAVID. It really doesn't seem to be here anywhere . . .

FRAZER. No.

SUSAN (*phone*). No, I told you at the time, there really isn't any point. How did you? How did you know where to . . . ?

FRAZER. Thing is, David . . . Susan sold it.

SUSAN (*phone*). No, I did not see you on the bus. I did not signal for you to get off and follow me, you're deluded. That's not . . . that's not so, I'm sorry.

Don't call me here again, I mean it.

SUSAN puts the phone down firmly and stuffs the roses into bin. Both DAVID and FRAZER watch amazed.

FRAZER. Hey, steady on, Susan.

SUSAN. Frazer, they were from You Know Who, I really don't want to discuss it, thank you!

FRAZER. Eh? – Oh right, from Mr Speed –

SUSAN. Frazer!

DAVID (*puzzled*). But could you not have . . . ? I mean, if you didn't want them?

SUSAN. What? Given them to charity?

SUSAN *fishes the roses back out of the bin.*

Yes, yes, of course, they're perfectly good roses, oh, only a little bit bashed and past it and worse for wear – do you want to buy them?

DAVID. No . . . just, sorry –

SUSAN. Sure? Because I could get Marjorie to give us a price. No? Oh well, they'll just have to go back in the bin – goodbye! – because if there's one thing worse than not getting flowers on Valentine's Day, it's getting flowers on Valentine's Day from someone who is the last person you'd ever want flowers off of on Valentine's Day, or any other.

FRAZER. We might have known, eh? How did he get the address?

SUSAN. I said I don't want to talk about it!

DAVID. Frazer says you sold it?

SUSAN. Does he?

SUSAN *glares at* FRAZER.

DORIS *comes out of the changing room with a garment*

DORIS. I'll take this, I suppose. There was nothing else. I've just left the rest all in there.

SUSAN. Fine, Doris.

DORIS *claps eyes on the ruby slippers on the counter. She flings the garment aside.*

DORIS. Oh here, look at these! These're lovely, leave that, I'll take them!

FRAZER. But, Doris, they'll no fit you!

DORIS. They will. Likely. What size are they, a four?

FRAZER. But they're awfully dear!

DORIS. A tenner! No for what they are.

SUSAN. Certainly, Doris, they're yours!

SUSAN *stuffs them into a bag takes the money from* DORIS *and rings it up. She thrusts the bag at* DORIS, *who exits, taking them, thoroughly delighted.*

DORIS (*to* DAVID *as she goes*). Cheeritata! Never let it be said your dancing days are over, eh?

DAVID. I mean, it's my own fault, totally. It is! Let me be the first to admit it. I'm an idiot, I really am. Careless! I brought them all over, these ties. Big clean sweep, you know? It was just that no sooner was I back in the door than I thought to myself, aaah!

I mean, I cannot believe I was so bloody stupid. Thoughtless.

My fault entirely!

Then I thought, well, I could go over, buy it back, but . . .

Listen, you wouldn't have any idea at all where the tie went?

MARJORIE *shouts out from backshop*

MARJORIE (*off*). No sign of it, David, I'm sorry!

DAVID (*calling*). Yes, yes, it's OK, Marjorie, thank you. (*To* SUSAN.) I mean, who bought it? Because if we could track them down, I could offer them double – more – to get it back?

I mean, I don't know if it's feasible at all, but . . . ?

(*Beat.*) Frazer, you don't happen to know, I don't suppose?

Who the tie was actually sold to?

FRAZER. Well . . . (*Beat.*) Susan, you don't think you –

SUSAN. No!

DAVID. You see, it's not the value of the thing, not at all, not the monetary value, what is it worth to anyone else but me and the person that made it, nothing, it's a handmade thing, you see, and it's not a question of would I ever wear it again or not – I probably wouldn't, that's absolutely not the point – the point is I really shouldn't have thrown it away, oh, I don't know if you've ever had a case before where somebody like me was silly enough to donate something they –

FRAZER. It happens all the time! Course it does.

Well, not all the time, no, but it happens, it does.

But we're usually lucky enough that they realise before we've actually sold it.

MARJORIE *enters*.

MARJORIE. No! No sign anywhere! So I'm pretty confident that in point of fact you never brought it, David, so check for us at home, eh?

DAVID. But this lady here sold it –

MARJORIE. No! That's quite impossible, because –

SUSAN. I did! I bloody sold the bloody thing! So don't you start either, Marjorie, I'm warning you. I used my gumption and I sold it for ten whole quid. I sold it! I looked at the stupid article and I thought: Valentine's Day, this is the day if ever there is a day you can sell this bloody hideous handmade-looking monstrosity; tomorrow and it'll be on the shelf for another year, she wants it, so sell it, so I sold it!

And, sorry, I'm not bloody sorry.

I work in here for sweet fanny nothing, for this charity, three days a week in good faith, out of nothing but the goodness of my heart, and I am sick, tired and fed up to the back teeth being treated like an idiot by idiots that run around after idiots that don't even know what they want to hand in and what crap they actually want to keep.

DAVID. It's just that it has sentimental value.

SUSAN. Does it? Present was it?

DAVID. Yes, as a matter of fact. You see, it's hand-painted on silk –

SUSAN. A present, very nice. From a young girl, I suppose?

DAVID (*puzzled and taken aback*). Well . . . She is just young, Helena, as a matter of fact . . .

SUSAN. How old?

DAVID. How – ?

SUSAN. Yes, Helena, how old?

DAVID. Twenty-one, no, twenty-two, but I really don't see –

SUSAN. Twenty-two? So you're what . . . Times two is forty-four plus seven – you're fifty one!

DAVID. I am! (How did you know?) I am. But –

SUSAN. And, David, you're a widower! David. Bet your wife wasn't six months in her grave before you were off cavorting with all the young Helenas of the day, typical! And now you want me to get my daughter – my innocent little fifteen-year-old daughter! – to steal some heart-spattered tie out of her estranged father's wardrobe just to get you out of a hole! Sure! Why not? I'll do it and we'll get it back for you, no bother, and I hope it chokes you!

SUSAN *marches off backshop in a rage. The other three stand amazed.*

MARJORIE. Well, poor Susan, she must be menopausal!

Blackout.

Music: 'My Funny Valentine'.

End of Act Two.

ACT THREE

HAVE YOURSELF A MERRY LITTLE CHRISTMAS
(*Tragi-comedy and Romance*)

Music: first verse of 'What is This Thing Called Love?' (Frank Sinatra version).

24 December, later that same year. The shop is now spectacularly spangled and decorated again, but very differently from the previous year. Though there is different tinsel and baubles, there is the same slightly sad, skew-whiff fairy on top of the (taller? more silvery?) Christmas tree.

A POLICEMAN talks on a crackling radio.

SUSAN sits shaking, wrapped in a blanket, head in hands.

The circling blue emergeny lights recede. Maybe a siren going away.

POLICEMAN. Fatality's name, a Robert Gilmartin, according to witness. Says you've got him on file. According to witness, he was under an injunction not to come near her because of reported harassment –

SUSAN (*blurts*). He was a stalker –

A young POLICEWOMAN comes from backshop with a steaming cup of tea for SUSAN.

POLICEWOMAN. Drink this.

SUSAN takes a drink and grimaces.

I know. It's very sweet. You've had a shock. Drink.

The POLICEWOMAN moves away from SUSAN, and the POLICEMAN continues on his radio, which crackles responses.

POLICEMAN. Yes. Taking full statement.

A Mrs Susan Love.

That's right. That's it. Yup.

No. No. Witness doesn't know next of kin or address herself, but says you'll definitely have it all.

Now, Mrs Love, can you tell me exactly what happened?

He gets his notebook out and SUSAN, *who takes a deep breath, begins.*

SUSAN. He came into the shop. Thing is, it's been kind of quiet recently on the Robert Gilmartin front. Comparatively. I was getting kind of lulled into a sense of false security. I thought perhaps he's getting the message, perhaps it's sinking in at last. Since I got the injunction I . . .

POLICEMAN. Is he your ex-husband? Or a former partner?

SUSAN. No. No. I don't even know him. I met him. Once. Once only, it was a . . . speed dating they called it, it was a . . . (*Peters out.*)

POLICEWOMAN. Oh I know! You get an equal number of men and women . . .

SUSAN. Yes, there's an organiser and she books the room and everything. After seven minutes the gong goes and the guys move round one place. It's like a Paul Jones. Well, I did this. Once. Almost a year ago. I'm divorced. Anyway, the one time I tried it . . .

POLICEMAN. Yes, could you – ?

SUSAN. Sorry! Robert Gilmartin was the last guy I met that night. I look back and I think it was only the luck of the draw but was it because I was the last woman he met and perhaps he was getting desperate? Anyway, I don't remember anything much about him. Was he weird? No weirder than some of the rest of them quite frankly.

Not interesting.

I knew I wasn't interested, but by then I was getting quite used to being pleasant enough, blah-blah, and the seven minutes'll be up soon, we can all go home.

That was that.

See, how it works is if there was anyone you wouldn't mind your details being passed on to, you tell the organiser –

Anyway, I got two or three e-mails from the organiser over the next month, a Robert Gilmartin wanted her to pass on his details to me although I hadn't singled him out, because he was sure I'd like to be in contact with him. I asked her to tell him very firmly, thanks but no thanks, and on no account to pass on mine.

POLICEWOMAN. And she did?

SUSAN. No, she didn't, it was just bad luck he saw me on the bus – I didn't see him, this was a good few weeks later, I wouldn't have recognised him if I did see him – and he followed me here. Then he followed me home. Once he had my address I was bombarded by flowers, presents I didn't want . . .

POLICEMAN. Did he threaten you?

SUSAN. No. No he didn't. But it was very threatening.

POLICEWOMAN. Of course.

POLICEMAN. They're not generally dangerous.

A look from the POLICEWOMAN.

SUSAN. And I was worried for my daughter too. He used to just stand there for hours. Across the street. Outside here as a matter of fact. All evening. Creepy. Outside this window. Looking up, looking over. Phoning. My dad has lived there for over forty years and had the same phone number, I had to change it, get a new unlisted number. It's been a nightmare. All year long. There was nothing I could say to get through to him. I had to let all the neighbours know on no account were they to . . . Humiliating. The police couldn't help much at first, but once I spoke to a female detective, she advised me, and I persevered and eventually I got the injunction. I could phone the police and they'd remove him. They did a couple of times. But sometimes I'd feel he'd never, ever, give up –

POLICEMAN. They do eventually.

SUSAN. Really?

The POLICEWOMAN *gives him a withering look. He witters, less confidently, a little deflated.*

POLICEMAN. Well, they are supposed to. Eventually. The ones who aren't violent. Or paranoid with jealousy and kill someone. (*Beat.*) That's the exes mainly.

SUSAN. Today he came into the shop – he must've been watching, he waited till I was alone – and said (*Breaking.*) he had a beautiful necklace he'd bought me for Christmas and we must spend the day together tomorrow, he knew I'd been sending him messages over his TV. I said I wasn't taking his present and if he left it, it was going in the bin and I dropped it straight in there in front of him and reminded him of the injunction and told him I was calling the police.

POLICEMAN. Is that it?

The POLICEMAN *retrieves a small parcel, nicely gift-wrapped, from a jewellers'.* SUSAN *flinches and shudders.*

SUSAN. Yes. Take it away. Take it away! Please!

POLICEWOMAN. Yes. It's all right. Ssh.

SUSAN. He said if I didn't agree to come with him for Christmas dinner . . . He said he was going to commit suicide.

(*Trembling.*) . . . And I said, 'Go right ahead, do what you want, it's nothing to do with me.'

The POLICEWOMAN *gets down to* SUSAN*'s level and gets direct eye contact.*

POLICEWOMAN (*gently*). And it isn't.

SUSAN. He's dead.

POLICEMAN. I don't think he really meant to do it, though. First bus driver said he ran right across his path looking right at him, dodging him and screaming. And straight into the other one coming the other way.

Poor guy never had a chance. That'll be his Christmas ruined!

The POLICEWOMAN *glares at him.*

SUSAN. A man's dead.

POLICEWOMAN. Can you go home? Is there anyone you can call to be with you?

SUSAN. No. No, I'll wait till the other two get back.

POLICEWOMAN. I really think you should call someone. Obviously you've had a hell of a shock –

SUSAN. But I didn't even know him . . .

POLICEMAN. She's right enough, you should go home.

SUSAN. I'm all right.

POLICEMAN. Well, we're off. And don't let it get to you, OK?

The POLICEMAN goes out of the front door. The POLICEWOMAN goes to exit with him then at the last minute comes back and pauses by SUSAN, crouches by her and says her piece.

POLICEWOMAN. Don't let this ruin your Christmas. He was a nutter, and yes, OK, it's a shame. Pity for him, but he's dead now and it's nothing – nothing – whatsoever to do with you. He didn't care about you. He didn't care about anyone but himself. Remember that.

The POLICEWOMAN goes. SUSAN sits, stricken, for a moment or two.

DAVID enters, smiling. She doesn't look up or register who he is.

DAVID. Hello, hello, err, is Frazer . . . ?

SUSAN. No.

DAVID. It's, eh, Susan, isn't it?

SUSAN (*flinching*). Oh you – !

As DAVID speaks, SUSAN gives tiny, almost imperceptible answers to his questions.

DAVID. Frazer phoned and left a message on the machine, said to pop in for a second, he had something to tell me that he thought would please me . . . ?

I'll come back later. Will he be in, could you tell him –
listen, are you OK?

No, you're not, are you?

You weren't a witness to that accident, were you?

Oh God. That's terrible, you don't think you should – are
you in here on your own?

SUSAN. Frazer will be back soon.

DAVID. Good. You didn't, eh, know the person . . . ?

Thank God for that.

The traffic's moving normally out there again as if nothing
had happened.

I was in a bus coming back from down the town and we
were just stuck in a big tailback for miles, took ages, finally
got here and I bumped into old Miss Llewelyn, my
downstairs neighbour, and she said what it was, there had
been a terrible accident.

SUSAN. Oh, do you know Margot Llewelyn?

DAVID. Stays downstairs. (*Beat.*) Are you sure you're OK?

SUSAN. Used to teach me piano when I was little. To no great
effect, I have to say. We stayed next door. Still do.

DAVID. Do you mean we're neighbours?

SUSAN. Number eighty-two. Just across the road there.

DAVID. Eighty-four. Just through the wall.

SUSAN. So you're the person plays all the loud jazz?
Specially on a Sunday morning?

DAVID. Sorry, does it disturb you?

SUSAN. No. I quite like it.

DAVID. So you're a jazz fan?

SUSAN. No.

DAVID. You'll be all right soon. I've just sold up. I'm moving
out in a fortnight. After twenty-six years. It was . . . Time
for a change.

SUSAN. Oh I didn't mean . . . I'll miss it. Sunday morning.

DAVID. It's weird though. I mean, cities are unbelievable, aren't they? So we've been neighbours all these years, presumably? Couldn't have been! Yet we've never met till I'm about to leave . . .

SUSAN. Oh no, no, I didn't stay there always. It's my dad's house. The family home. We moved in when I was seven, I left home at eighteen when I went to university, so . . .

My daughter and I moved back in nearly two years ago when Dad was beginning to not cope.

DAVID. Your dad is Archie Dickinson of Dickinson the Plumbers, isn't he?

SUSAN. Do you know him?

DAVID. Put in our new bathroom when we moved in in 1978. I've certainly seen him out and about locally over the years.

SUSAN. My dad went into a home at the beginning of this month. He's so confused and I was scared to death of him just wandering off and going missing ...

I just couldn't cope any more and the social worker said . . . And suddenly a place came up . . . And I put him in.

DAVID. That's not how to think of it. It must've been time.

Not Rylands, is it?

SUSAN. Yes.

DAVID. My mother's been in there for four-and-a-half years. It's very pleasant as these places go. They're very, very good. They really are.

SUSAN. Oh God, I hope so. (*Beat.*) Mr . . .

DAVID. David.

SUSAN. Listen, why Frazer phoned you . . . I think what it must have been . . . I know it's been ages, but better late than never, eh? . . . I got back your tie.

She begins with increasing puzzlement then panic to search through a drawer in the counter.

DAVID. My tie, that I . . . ?

SUSAN. I told him to wait till after Christmas, till after I left. Then return it!

This is my last day.

I've got a new job, a proper job that I start on the fifth of January and I . . . Well, getting that tie back I'd no right selling in the first place . . . that was sort of a bit of unfinished business, and I . . . never mind, I retrieved it last week and I asked Frazer to let you . . . And I put it in the drawer here, I did! And somebody's moved it.

She's nearly crying.

DAVID. Don't get upset, honestly – it'll no doubt turn up.

SUSAN *takes a deep breath.*

SUSAN. David, I've only met you once, all those months and months ago, and I was unforgiveably rude to you. It was unbelievable, it really was, and I don't know how to apologise and I certainly couldn't begin to explain why you, a total stranger, got it in the neck like that.

DAVID. Susan – I can call you Susan? – it's OK. Frazer explained.

You weren't having a good day, were you, to put it mildly, and then this idiot comes in, wanting something back you've already sold in good faith –

SUSAN. But I was totally out of order.

DAVID. You were a bit!

But you were very good value. You really made me laugh. It was very, very funny, Susan.

SUSAN. No.

DAVID. I couldn't take it personally, well, you didn't even know me. I was quite taken aback, I must admit. I just stood there. Then all of a sudden it just cracked me up.

Oh, you should've seen Marjorie's face.

SUSAN. Don't.

DAVID. It was a picture, it really was!

He begins to laugh. Eventually she joins in.

And you got the right answer by the wrong method! The Maths teacher in me would have to give you no marks for that.

SUSAN. Sorry . . . ?

DAVID. You said I was fifty-one. Correct. I am. Fifty-two next month, actually, but who's counting? Frazer explained your theory – well, leaving aside the doubtful premise it's based on – purely as arithmetic, you can't double the woman's age and add seven, you'd have to deduct seven from the woman's age then double that figure, so the age of the man whose ideal woman is twenty-two is twenty-two minus seven equals fifteen, times two is thirty. Not fifty-one.

SUSAN. Oh, right enough.

DAVID. Right enough, I'm right!

SUSAN. Is that what you are?

DAVID. What?

SUSAN. A Maths teacher.

DAVID. Uh-huh! And you?

SUSAN. Office administrator. (*Beat.*) This new job I've got sounds pretty challenging . . .

DAVID. Well, good! I'm sure you'll rise to it!

SUSAN. I hope so.

DAVID. Course you will!

SUSAN. I'm looking forward to it. Nervous of course. Where do you teach?

DAVID. Just round the corner at the high school.

SUSAN. My daughter goes there.

DAVID. What's her name?

SUSAN. Stephanie Love.

DAVID. I know Stephanie! Super girl, I don't actually teach her but she was one of the group I took on the trip to Paris at Easter.

SUSAN. So you're . . . ? Oh, I heard all about it, what great laughs it all was. There was you and Miss . . .

DAVID – Collins from the Art Department, and Mrs Copeland from French, it was quite an education!

SUSAN. I thought it was fantastic you all giving up your holidays like that. I don't think I would.

DAVID. Well . . . the extra-curricular stuff can be really quite rewarding. They were a good gang, that lot. And Paris, anytime . . . !

I actually enjoy my work. I like teaching. I like teaching Maths. It's great when you can actually see the penny drop.

Oh, it's got its humdrum elements of course, nowadays there is the hooligan factor even in a basically really good school like ours – and the admin is a nightmare . . . but there've been times in my life when going to my work and taking pride in doing an honest day at the chalkface's been just about the only thing to hold everything together for me.

SUSAN. Are you not going to be the new headmaster?

DAVID. Me? No, God forbid!

SUSAN. Can't imagine there're that many Maths teachers turning up at work in the Jon Snow fancy ties!

DAVID. Oh, you mean the –

SUSAN. I'm sure it'll just be Frazer's put it somewhere safe, David. He knew how important that tie was to you.

DAVID. And to you! After all, you went to the effort of getting it back for me. Susan, I'm very, very –

Enter HELENA, *seen just in silhouette, a good-looking twenty-two-year-old with a Czech accent and an absolutely huge 'just-about-to-drop' pregnant bump.*

HELENA. David!

DAVID. (Hey! Don't mention the tie to her! OK?)

HELENA. There you are! I need you at home!

Exit HELENA.

DAVID. Sorry, Helena! Oh, I'm sorry, darling! I'll only be a minute, I'm just coming!

It'd have been really nice to wear it at Christmas dinner and please her but, oh well!

Everybody gets into such a lather this time of the year, don't they? Trying to get everything perfect. And she's such a driven kind of a girl at the best of times and what with the pregnancy –

SUSAN. Had you not better go?

DAVID. I suppose so! Susan, take care, eh? And see and have a nice Christmas. Hey! If I don't bump into you again before the Big Move, it was nice knowing you!

DAVID *exits.*

SUSAN *sits down, utterly deflated.*

SUSAN. Oh yes, of course! City flats are murder with a pram, eh? Well, wherever you're going, here's hoping you've got a garden!

Enter TONY.

TONY. Susan.

SUSAN. Tony.

TONY. Listen, Susan, I think our Stephi would be willing to come home to you.

SUSAN. Oh really, well, that's not the response I got from her when I phoned her at your place last week.

TONY. Well, she's stubborn and I know she was still keeping up the huff with you, but I happen to know she was crying her eyes out last night and –

SUSAN. And you and Natalie would like to have your first Christmas at home alone with Baby Whatsit without a stroppy adolescent to entertain, I don't blame you.

TONY. Susan, why do you always have to take a dim view?

Of every single thing I try to do. Of every single gesture I try to make?

I'd like you not to be on your own. And I thought you'd like her to be there. With you. At Christmas. And – oh, she'd never admit it – but I know she'd like to come home. Particularly once she found out that Natalie and I are even stricter with the time she's to be in at than you are.

SUSAN. You'd like me to have company at Christmas? That's rich! Thanks a lot. I'm really grateful for your concern.

He holds out his arms in a gesture of surrender.

TONY. Ah, c'mon, Susan . . .

They look each other in the eye. A beat.

SUSAN. Do you love her, Tony?

TONY. You know fine well I'm crazy about our Stephi, always have been.

SUSAN. No. No, I meant Natalie?

Do you love her, Tony? Do you love her to bits?

TONY. Yes. Yes I do.

SUSAN. Well, that's good because I'd hate for all that agony and turmoil to have been for nothing.

TONY. It's not easy, not always easy to be a new dad at my age, and – (*Catching on to himself, laughing.*) – but I don't suppose you want to be hearing that?

SUSAN (*wry laugh*). Not particularly, my reserves of sympathy remain very finite.

TONY. Fair enough.

Enter DAVID.

DAVID. Susan –

SUSAN. No, Mr . . . erm, Frazer's not back yet! I *will* get him to call you the minute he does and here's hoping he can shed some light on the mystery, OK? We'll do our very best for you! Bye bye just now!

DAVID *is forced to give in, make a goodbye gesture and exit.*

TONY. Who's that?

SUSAN. Just a guy that comes into the shop.

So, Tony, you're saying I should try again? To phone Stephi?

TONY. Let me talk to her on her mobile. I'll get her to call you.

SUSAN. OK.

They smile amicably enough at each other, and he goes to exit. But at the last moment he has to blow it with a provocative question.

TONY. Susan, why did you fight with her over that top she wanted to wear to the school dance? It's just what they're all wearing, it really is. Natalie says –

SUSAN. Tony, I didn't fall out with her about the skimpy top, I didn't fall out with her going to the school dance like a cross between a teenage hooker and something out of *Sex and the City*, I didn't fall out with her about the pierced navel or the temporary tattoo or the sequined thong showing right out over the top of the skintight hipsters cut low enough to practically show her entire 'excuse me'. I maybe don't get out much but somehow, by some sort of osmosis, I do seem to know what is de rigeur for fifteen-year-olds these days.

I fell out with her because she wouldn't wear a coat, Tony.

To go to the dance. In December, Tony.

TONY *is laughing at the old SUSAN. She's good value. She always was.*

TONY. Well, it's all water under the bridge now. And if you just don't mention it and she thinks you'd like her to come back – I told her I'd ask you if she could come back, Susan.

SUSAN. Well, of course she can.

SUSAN *is nearly managing a smile now too. They look each other in the eye. TONY tries an awkward 'bye bye' peck on the cheek, but it doesn't go quite right.*

TONY. Have a good Christmas, eh, the two of you, and all the best.

SUSAN. We'll see.

TONY. I do wish you all the best.

Another flash of bitterness from SUSAN, *surprising herself.*

SUSAN. Of course you do, and you'd like to see me happy because you could stop feeling guilty.

TONY. But I don't, actually. Waste of time. Guilt. Regrets. Load of crap.

Susan . . . I never really felt you were on my side.

SUSAN. No? No, I suppose I wasn't always. Not latterly.

TONY. All the best. Really.

SUSAN. Yeah. (*Beat.*) You too.

As he goes to exit:

Tony!

Thanks for sending back that tie to the shop when I asked you.

TONY. No problem, Susan. No bother at all.

Exit TONY. SUSAN *alone for a beat, thinking, feeling.*

Enter MARJORIE *through the front door in coat with bags. She's very hyped up and breathless about Christmas.*

MARJORIE. That dear delicatessen is queues around the block! Well, Christmas Eve, what would you expect, I suppose?

MARJORIE *bustles into backshop, then back out again, minus her coat and packages.*

Was that Tony I saw leaving?

What did that so-and-so want coming in here?

SUSAN. Nothing.

To wish me a happy Christmas.

MARJORIE. Damnable cheek!

MARJORIE *begins to ricochet about the shop fussing with things and rattling on so much she leaves no space for a response.*

I popped in to Scandalrags to see if they had anything suitable for the Golf Club Dinner Dance and the woman was telling me there had been a terrible accident!

Course, I had to miss everything because I was round the corner in that queue.

Christmas. It'll be no bloody Christmas for me. Skivvying around after a brood of ungrateful articles and every time I get interested in something on the telly (mind you, there's damn all on) some so-and-so switches the channel!

Last night I'd just finished the tree, and Douglas had managed to fuse the lights as per usual, so I just tried to calm myself by putting a little bit of effort into my festive flowers and I'd done a beautiful arrangement – though I say it myself, you know asymmetric with a twisty twig? – and I had just placed it just so, perfect, on the hall table and stepped back to admire it, when – blam! – a bloody great football comes crashing along the hall and smacks straight into it, broken porcelain, bashed blossoms and water all over the parquet. I sat down and I cried buckets.

That's a brood of boys for you.

Darling, are you just going to sit there in a dream all day?

MARJORIE *stands and stares out the window, lost in her own world, quite unaware of* SUSAN *behind her.*

Oh, look, there's Doris! Looks like she's got on a new brassiere. Och aye the noo!

Wonder if she's coming in? Yes, yes, here she comes, no, no, as you were, she's not, she's gone by. Thank goodness.

It'd take blinking Scotch Doris to come in and annoy us on Christmas Eve, eh? I think I'm going to pop a little note to Head Office next year, there's not much point in us actually opening, the amount of trade we get.

I hate Christmas.

Take last year. Practically had to sleep with the butcher to get on his list for a Kelly Bronze, you know, that's that breed of free-range turkey Delia swears by – an arm and a leg, extortionate – so I thought: 'Live up to the bird, I better pull out the stops stuffing-wise', so down with the Cuisinart and it's the cook-and-peel-your-own chestnuts, the home-made minced pork belly, the Perigord, the Pernod, I don't know what, and it's sitting there ready in the fridge in a bowl with the teacloth over it, I come down Christmas morning and it's empty. Stephen's come back in at midnight with half the rugby first fifteen, turned it into hamburger patties and they've scoffed the lot on buns with tomato ketchup! All I got was, 'Mum, we'd the munchies.' The munchies! He says, 'Mum, these burgers, they were mingers.' Scrimp and scrape to send them to a good school and they still talk like I don't know what!

So that was us reduced to the packet of Paxo sage and onion, and to add insult to injury, Douglas had to say that was his favourite bit of the meal, reminded him of how his old mum used to make it.

Plus Marcus my youngest has decided he's a lacto-veggie and will eat absolutely bugger all but soya sausages –

SUSAN *sinks to the floor, beginning to scream and cry.*

Enter FRAZER.

FRAZER. Guy in the Asian grocer's told me there'd been a terrible acci –

SUSAN *flies into his arms, crying. He comforts her.*

MARJORIE. Tell you, it'll be that blinking nuisance of an ex-husband upsetting her, Frazer, because when I came in –

SUSAN (*sobbing*). It was Robert Gilmartin! And he's dead.

MARJORIE *and* FRAZER *are stunned.*

MARJORIE. Through here! Come on! Through here! A cup of tea and half a Valium, that's what you're needing, dear.

FRAZER *and* MARJORIE *help a practically prostrate* SUSAN *through to backshop.*

DAVID *enters and looks around puzzled.*

DAVID. Hello? Hello?

MARJORIE *enters from backshop, firmly shutting the door with its private sign.*

MARJORIE. Hello! Oh, it's you David, I'm afraid we're a little bit busy.

DAVID. Marjorie. Erm, I was wondering if I could see Susan, please.

MARJORIE. No, that's just it, she's a little bit indisposed at the moment.

DAVID. But I'd just –

Enter FRAZER *from backshop.*

FRAZER. David! I came by your house and rang the bell half an hour ago but no answer.

MARJORIE. How is she, Frazer?

FRAZER. Well, this is it, Marjorie, I don't like the colour of her at all.

DAVID *goes to the private door,* MARJORIE *bars his way.*

DAVID. If I could just –

MARJORIE (*briskly*). No certainly not, David, we'll pass on any message you've got for her –

DAVID. But I just want to –

FRAZER. Here, David! I've got your tie! (Go away through, Marjorie, and see what you think. I said to her, perhaps we should call a doctor, but she'll not have it.)

MARJORIE *exits backshop.* FRAZER *pulls the tie out of his pocket, hands it over to* DAVID.

Put it in my pocket when I went out there, and I thought I'll just see if I can deliver it in person.

Susan said she'd been feeling guilty all these months about not getting it back for you.

DAVID. No need whatsoever, I was –

FRAZER. I thought you'd be delighted!

DAVID. Well, I am, I am, but –

MARJORIE (*calling from backshop*). Frazer!

FRAZER. Excuse me just a little minute, David –

DAVID. Frazer. Could you ask Susan if she'd like a lift up to Rylands tomorrow? Because I'm going up to see my mother and she was telling me about her dad . . . I don't know if she drives, but –

FRAZER. No, Susan's not got a car, no.

DAVID. Well, it can be hard to get a taxi on Christmas Day and –

FRAZER. That's awfully kind of you, David, but I've already arranged to pop round in the car at eleven and take her up. It's no bother. I'm not doing hellish much anyway!

DAVID. Oh, well, I just thought –

FRAZER. There's honestly no need.

DAVID. But could you tell her – ?

FRAZER. Have a merry Christmas, David! Excuse me, will you?

FRAZER *exits backshop.*

DAVID *looks at the heart-spattered tie and glumly puts it on in a mirror. It certainly doesn't go with his casual tartan shirt. He pretends to hang himself with it. He sighs, gives up (he's forced to, really), and exits through the front door.*

SUSAN *enters from backshop pursued by* MARJORIE *with a glass of water and a pill, and by* FRAZER.

SUSAN. No, Marjorie, I don't want a pill, honestly! I'm fine now!

MARJORIE. You've had a terrible shock!

SUSAN. Poor guy!

Love. A fatal carry-on. Madness. You wouldn't wish it on your worst enemy.

I remember, oh, two or three years before I met Tony I was
in love, mad unrequited love, with a guy called Arthur.
Arthur! Ridiculous. Once I stood outside his flat for a whole
weekend – it was freezing as well – because I knew he was
in there with a girl called Heather Maxwell instead of on a
works weekend like he'd said he was. And thing was, I
knew he really loved me, he just hadn't realised it yet.

I was, looking back – really – in myself – just every bit as
nuts as Robert Gilmartin.

I really never do want to go there again.

Never again will I try any of these . . . You were right,
Frazer, it was desperate, and if you do desperate things, it
puts you in touch with desperate people.

Love? Spare me! No, what I want most of all is peace.

MARJORIE. I think you're very wise, Susan. Live for
yourself. Have things exactly the way you want them.

I'll tell you, see, if it wasn't for Douglas and the boys, I'd
have a pink fitted carpet in the bathroom.

Because the male aim is only ninety per cent accurate, isn't
it? If that.

SUSAN. It's a terrible thing to say but I'm glad it's all over.

MARJORIE. If you'll not take a little half a Valium, Susan, I'll
tell you, I'm going to pop out to get you some Sleepy-Time
Tea out the health-food shop, make sure you sleep tonight.
Celia who works in here on a Tuesday swears by it.

MARJORIE *goes backshop from there.*

Frazer, kettle's boiling!

But FRAZER *stands still, staring strangely at* SUSAN.

MARJORIE *bustles out from backshop in her coat* –

That and I'll get you some St John's Wort when I'm at it,
it's wonderful for getting you through the winter, so it is,
and it's not drugs, dear, it's only herbal.

– *and she hurries out the front door. As she goes:*

Frazer! Are you not going to make that tea?

FRAZER *rouses himself and goes backshop. The moment he's off,* SUSAN*'s mobile rings with a daft ringtone. She answers quickly, eagerly, the tiny phone clapped against her left ear.*

SUSAN. Oh, Stephi! Stephi, your dad said he'd get you to phone. Come home, love!

OK.

No, no of course I've not got a tree, why would I bother a tree for just me?

OK, OK, I'm saying nothing, I'm listening.

FRAZER *enters, launching straight into it as he does.*

FRAZER. I'm not even going to look at you till I get it out but I might as well say it before Marjorie gets back because it's something I've wanted to say for a while, I suppose. Am I wrong to hope that perhaps one day you and me might get married?

I mean, once sex is out of the equation.

Because Marjorie's perhaps decided I'm gay, but I'm not. If I think of what it is to be gay, it makes me shudder, it does, the whole lifestyle. Plus my mother would've had a fit and I suppose her attitude's rubbed off on me and I like women. I really like you, Susan, and I always have and do we not get on like a house on fire?

SUSAN (*on the phone*). Oh, darling, I don't know what I'd do with myself if it came to you and me not getting on!

FRAZER. Face facts, Frazer, you're not a 'costume designer', you're not going back to London – I hated London, I was over the moon to scuttle back home and look after Mother. I'm a part-time dog walker, and a part-time gardener, and a part-time volunteer in a charity shop and, oh yes, I'll run up a lovely frock for a mother of the bride for a very reasonable price in jigtime.

And I get by.

Except it's a little bit lonely at times and if I have a dream – don't laugh, Susan –

SUSAN, *on the phone, lets out a loud snort then a peal of laughter, then —*

SUSAN. Oh, you take the biscuit, Stephi, you really do. OK, it's a deal, see you later, baby!

She clicks off the phone and goes, smiling happily, to FRAZER.

The prodigal returns! Tonight about teatime.

Only snag is she's booked the very last tree in the Asian grocer's and she and her boyfriend – this is a new development! – are going to bring it up and get down the decorations and do it up in the living room – from which I am banned for the evening, poor old Cinders here's got her full instructions on what kind of pizza to be putting in the oven for them in the kitchen –

Sorry, Frazer, were you saying something?

FRAZER *sits, shattered, but she doesn't notice, so ecstatic is she about Stephi.*

Enter DORIS, *dressed in her usual outfit but with an infrastructure giving her an oddly altered, uplifted bosom and carrying a bundle of three peculiarly wrapped presents in a string bag. She picks up a twee little dish from among the merchandise on display.*

DORIS. That's nice! It's a bonny wee dish, that, intit?

SUSAN. Very nice! I think it's Dutch, Doris. Delft.

DORIS. Dutch Delft? Is it? (*Unimpressed.*) You don't say.

Haw, Susan, what kind of a dish would you cry that wee dish?

SUSAN. Dunno. Just a dish . . .

DORIS. Whit fur?

SUSAN. Well . . . Frazer . . . ?

FRAZER (*shrugs*). A little bonbon dish, basically.

DORIS. A bonbon dish? It's bonny.

Like for nuts or that?

SUSAN. Exactly.

DORIS. It's nice. Perhaps I should buy myself that bonny wee bonbon dish for my Christmas?

SUSAN. Go on, Doris, make our day! Why don't you be our sole customer and make us feel we've not been totally wasting our time. Tell you, how about a pre-Christmas sale, it's marked at a pound – let's say seventy per cent off –30p to you.

DORIS. It's no dear.

SUSAN. It is not.

DORIS. And it is bonny.

SUSAN. It is.

DORIS. Mind you, I've already got enough blinking crap and tat at home. A houseful of bloody rubbish! Gloryholes stuffed to the gunnels with gash this that and the next thing. Shite coming out my ears.

So I'll not bother, so I willnae.

Why I came in, a little bird told me you were leaving.

SUSAN. I am, Doris. A paying job presented itself so . . .

DORIS. Good things come to those that wait!

All the best, hen.

SUSAN. Thank you very much!

DORIS. So I wanted to leave you a little minding.

DORIS *takes three bizarre parcels out of her string bag.*

SUSAN. Oh-ho, don't worry, Doris, I'll not forget you.

DORIS. And seeing it's Christmas . . . I've brung in something for Frazer and Marjorie as well. I'd that much re-fankled recycled paper, I thought I might as well yase some o it up.

DORIS *leaves these three presents – one clearly a bottle; one obviously a vinyl LP record; one a lumpy, amorphous ball of a parcel with a great big label reading 'Susan'.*

SUSAN. Thank you very much, Doris, honestly, you really shouldn't –

DORIS. No, don't unwrap them, it's no Christmas yit! I'm away. I'm away up the community centre to the carol concert, you get a lovely tea after with hoat mince pies. All the best, eh?

All the best when it comes.

Exit DORIS.

SUSAN. Well, there's a turn-up for the books, eh?

Doris. One thing you'd have to admit, she's totally unpredictable.

Wonder what we got?

Gold, frankincense and myrrh? Possibly not!

No prize for guessing what's in yours, Frazer!

A bottle. (*She feels it.*) Oh well, a bottle of what, that's the sixty-four-thousand-dollar question!

Erm . . . A bottle of Doris's own home-made elderberry wine decanted into an old turpentine bottle?

Ermm . . . A bottle of very fusty crème de menthe?

A bottle of bath-oil circa 1965?

An absolutely ancient bottle of Beaujolais Nouveau?

A ship in a bottle!

A message in a bottle –

Sorry. Sorry, Frazer, were you saying something there? Before Doris came in? When I was on the phone to Stephi?

FRAZER. No. No, nothing important, Susan, I can't remember. Doesn't matter.

SUSAN. Will we open them? Early? Put ourselves in the mood. Oh, why not? Why not indeed, give ourselves a

laugh, eh? What have we got, for goodness' sake? God
knows!

Marjorie's is definitely the size and the feel of an LP.

Remember getting an LP for your Christmas, Frazer? Sorry,
album! I'm showing my age, eh? Big time.

Will we? Because she said not till –

FRAZER. Oh, open yours! Go on.

SUSAN. Nah. You first . . .

FRAZER *hums 'The Stripper' tune, and disrobes his bottle
of its paper, layer by layer. By now they are laughing.
Eventually, out comes a bottle of very nice indeed, thank
you, champagne. They are amazed.*

FRAZER. Cold too! Well, well!

Enter DAVID. *The heart tie is still very, very loosely
knotted round his neck, incongruous with the tartan shirt.*

DAVID. That looks very nice. Christmas starting early?

SUSAN (*of tie, amazed*). Oh, you got it?

DAVID. I came in. Frazer not tell you?

SUSAN. No!

FRAZER. Oh, I haven't had the time!

SUSAN. Sorry, we've just had surprise Christmas presents
from our favourite never-satisfied customer!

Enter MARJORIE *who puts down a little package from the
health-food store in front of* SUSAN.

MARJORIE. Just in time, they were closing up. There we are,
Susan, those'll sort you. Ooh . . . I think it's about time we
shut up shop ourselves?

SUSAN. Look, Marjorie, Doris left a present for you.

MARJORIE. Scotch Doris? For goodness' sake, I shouldn't
have waved to her earlier, I obviously only encouraged her.

SUSAN. Open it up! Go on!

MARJORIE. All right, if you say so. (*Opens it.*) Oh, a record. It's all CDs nowadays, isn't it?

DAVID. Not necessarily!

DAVID takes it from her, blows on it looks at it in the light.

It's old, yes. But it looks as if it's in OK nick . . .

FRAZER. That turntable's in working order you know, we let people try them out on it if they want.

But DAVID hands it back to MARJORIE who looks at it disdainfully.

MARJORIE (*reading*). *Christmas Classics*? Well, that can join the junk mountain . . .

DAVID (*quietly, to SUSAN and FRAZER*). Listen, why I came over, I wondered if I could invite you pair, well, it's awfully short notice I know, you'll very likely both be busy, but tonight we're having Christmas dinner in our house, and . . .

My daughter-in-law Helena – you met her earlier, Susan – she's Czech you know, and there they do Christmas dinner on Christmas Eve apparently, they make baked carp, it's the Christmas fish and . . . oh, it's traditional, and Colin – that's my son – the pair of them are visiting, anyway, he says it's the being pregnant has made Helena mad to do everything absolutely just so the Czech way for once, and it's very much the more the merrier. Old Margot Llewelyn has even promised to brave the stairs.

SUSAN. Helena's your daughter-in-law?

DAVID. Of course! Susan, you didn't think . . .

He begins to laugh. She's embarassed.

You shouldn't believe everything you read in magazines. Really!

Yes, the famous tie was part of the wedding outfits. Helena had a coat lined with this fabric, she made it herself, and she made us all wear matching ties. Colin, the best man, her father, me.

She did Textile Design at art school.

MARJORIE. So you're going to be a grandad, David?

DAVID. I am.

MARJORIE. Not make you feel old?

DAVID. Not really! I'm delighted.

Are you busy tonight, Marjorie, because, of course, you're very welcome to –

MARJORIE. Goodness me, no, David, thank you, but no thanks, my family are all-consuming this time of year.

DAVID. Of course, so . . . ?

FRAZER. I'm actually busy, David, sorry.

DAVID (*genuinely*). Oh, that's a disappointment.

Susan? Helena's a terrific cook, I'll guarantee you that.

SUSAN. Well . . . (*Laughs.*) I was reconciled to dining on the crumbs from someone's pizza, so –

DAVID. Lovely. About, say, half past seven for drinks . . . ?

FRAZER, *making a big effort to be generous, wields his bottle.*

FRAZER. Why don't we have this now?

MARJORIE. Ooh . . . Why not? Teensy one for me though, Frazer, I'm driving.

FRAZER. Hurry up and open your Doris doofer, Suze, you'll perhaps have the plum duff. Lay on McDuff!

SUSAN *begins to unwrap her lump of a present.*
MARJORIE *picks up a boxed set of champagne flute glasses from among the merchandise.*

MARJORIE. I might as well give these a little rinse and we'll use them, eh?

FRAZER. But Marjorie! They're stock! And they're still in the box!

MARJORIE. Frazer, don't be so bloody stupid. It's Christmas!

And she slips off with them to backshop.

DAVID. And we should surely try the music while we're at it?

DAVID picks up MARJORIE's LP and sets about putting it on the turntable. He calls through to her.

May I, Marjorie?

MARJORIE (*off*). Sorry, David?

SUSAN. Frazer, look!

SUSAN, finishing unwrapping her present, astonished, holds out the 'ruby slippers'.

Then claps her hand to her mouth, remembering their provenance. But DAVID, having set the needle in the record's groove and waiting for the music to start, turns and looks on in absolute equanimity.

DAVID. They're lovely. Are they going to fit?

The record begins, the first line of 'Have Yourself a Merry Little Christmas'. SUSAN nods solemnly.

SUSAN (*hushed*). I think so . . . Yes.

FRAZER. Go on, Susan! Put them on!

She slips them on. DAVID throws off his jacket, turns and very deliberately straightens his tie, tightening the knot.

DAVID. Let's dance.

He holds out his arms, and shyly, tentatively, awkwardly at first, SUSAN and DAVID begin to dance.

FRAZER, left out, sighs one single small audible breath.

MARJORIE (*calling from backshop*). Frazer, Frazer! Give me a hand with this tray, can't you?

FRAZER (*a beat*). Coming Marjorie, coming, I'm all yours.

He exits backshop, flourishing the bottle of champagne.

Alone, still awkwardly, SUSAN and DAVID waltz.

The record – well, it was a present from half-cracked DORIS – begins to reveal an increasingly intrusive scratch and a click as it plays.

They laugh heartily, joyfully, at this audible crack, looking into each others eyes. At this moment, indoors as it is, magical snow begins to fall.

They close in and dance on together.

The End..